Discover the world's best destinations with the Insight Guides Walking Eye app, available to download for free in the App Store and Google Play.

The container app provides easy access to fantastic free content on events and activities taking place in your current location or chosen destination, with the possibility of booking, as well as the regularly-updated Insight Guides travel blog: Inspire Me. In addition, you can purchase curated, premium destination guides through the app, which feature local highlights, hotel, bar, restaurant and shopping listings, an A to Z of practical information and more. Or purchase and download Insight Guides eBooks straight to your device.

TOP 10 ATTRACTIONS

THE BIG SHOT AT THE STRATOSPHERE
A must for thrill seekers. See page 48.

BELLAGIO
The spectacular fountains in front of this lavish casino-resort make it an unmissable attraction. See page 41.

HIGH ROLLER
The world's biggest Ferris wheel offers spectacular views of The Strip. See page 43.

THE FREMONT STREET EXPERIENCE
With over 2 million lights, it's neon nirvana. See page 54.

LAS VEGAS
POCKET GUIDE

HOOVER DAM
A marvel of 1930s engineering. See page 63.

THE LUXOR
This resort is housed in a huge pyramid. See page 32.

CITYCENTER
Sleek and modern, this is a city within the city. See page 37.

THE CHANDELIER
A three-story bar, designed to make patrons feel like they're inside a chandelier. See page 38.

BINION'S GAMBLING HALL
Downtown casinos offer the best value, and this place is among the best. See page 54.

GRAND CANYON NATIONAL PARK
One of the wonders of the natural world, and just an excursion away from Vegas. See page 69.

A PERFECT DAY

9.30am

Breakfast
Start the day with a great buffet breakfast, either at your hotel or from the lavish menu at the Wynn's Tableau restaurant.

2.45pm

Spa luxury
Spas in Las Vegas are always jockeying for the title of best in show. The undisputed champion: Qua Baths & Spa inside Caesars Palace. Master barber offers men old-school flat-razor shaves, while women love to luxuriate in the Roman Baths after indulgent signature treatments such as the exfoliation body scrub or a hot-stone massage.

10.30am

Shop till you drop
Break out the credit cards for a dose of retail therapy at the Miracle Mile Shops inside Planet Hollywood or at the LINQ Promenade.

1.00pm

Lunch and people-watch
The open-air patio of Mon Ami Gabi, at Paris Las Vegas, is a great spot to linger over a lunch of croque-monsieur. It's also a good spot from which to watch hundreds of people as they wander down the Strip, or ogle at the fountains at Bellagio across the street.

5.00pm

Drinks with a view
Clean up and continue the Zen vibe from the 23rd floor of the Mandarin Oriental at the Mandarin Bar. The view in both directions of the Strip is amazing, and the sparkling wine is almost exclusively from France. Be sure to try some hors d'oeuvres, too.

.30pm

urrender to sweets

ecline dessert at SW Steakhouse and instead take
n evening walk north along the Strip to Luv-It Frozen
ustard, a legendary spot near the Stratosphere,
erving delicious sundaes.

1.00am

Party all night long

The hottest nightclub
in town is Marquee at
The Cosmopolitan. The
joint jumps with parties
raging indoors and out.
Views abound throughout
the venue, and house
music never sounded
so good (or loud). When
you've had enough of the
bump-and-grind, head to
Vesper Bar near the hotel
lobby for modern spins
on classic cocktails.

.30pm

teakhouse feast

ail a taxi to Wynn Las
egas, get out near the
Wynn Tower Suites,
nd stroll through the
Wynn's gardens as
ou make your way
hrough the covered
assageway to Encore.
our destination: SW
Steakhouse, where chef
David Walzog cooks an
utstanding American
steakhouse fare.

10.30pm

Press the felt

Professional poker players come from all over the
world to push all-in at the poker room inside Bellagio.
Even if you don't play, it's a great place to watch the
true high-rollers.

CONTENTS

INTRODUCTION

Only 100 years ago, Las Vegas was no more than a dusty railroad stop in the middle of an unforgiving desert valley. Dramatic changes occurred in the valley throughout the 20th century to create this fantasy, known today as the 'Entertainment Capital of the World', resulting in a city of mythic proportion and impossible illusion.

Initially settled in the mid-1800s, Las Vegas struggled as an isolated outpost for much of its early existence. The meager settlement was only declared a town in 1905. That year, on May 15, officials from the San Pedro, Los Angeles & Salt Lake Railroad auctioned 1,200 parcels of land mapping 40 square blocks in the desert dust. Within a year, the city's population grew to 1,500 brave pioneers.

LANDMARKS OF THE MODERN WORLD

Today's visitors are greeted by the fastest-growing, most rapidly changing city in the American West. They mingle and play among iconic landmarks of the world's great cities: replicas of the Eiffel Tower, the skyscrapers of Manhattan, the palaces of ancient Rome, and an Egyptian pyramid loom along the Strip to entrance and entice.

Today you'll see very little trace of the features that spawned and nurtured the fledgling city – its natural springs, most of which have long since run dry. Though water flows freely through the artificial lakes, swimming pools, and famous dancing fountains, it now comes in a giant pipeline from the Colorado River. Without that pipeline, the city would dry up and crumble back into the desert.

FAST LANE

Las Vegas is located in Clark County, Nevada, near the southern tip of the state. Clark County has more than 2.1

million inhabitants, and nearly 620,000 of them reside in Las Vegas. Nevada, which ranks as the seventh largest state by area, has a total of about 2.8 million inhabitants, making it only the 35th most populous state. There is a great deal of space in Nevada, but most of the people can be found in one tiny corner. Nevada is one of the fastest-growing states in the US; between 2010 and 2014 its population increased by over 5 percent.

SUNNY DAYS

Las Vegas has an average of just four inches (10cm) of rainfall and 310 days of sunshine each year. Summers are hot, with temperatures often nearing 115°F (46°C). In winter, daytime temperatures can be a pleasant 65°F (18°C), but nights can be quite cold, dropping all the way down to 34°F (1°C). Early spring and late fall are the best times to visit,

An aerial view of Las Vegas Strip

as the days are warm and the nights comfortably cool. In the height of summer, the casinos, hotels, and restaurants can be quite cool, as the air-conditioning blasts away to keep the heat at bay.

RUSH TO THE NEW

Las Vegas is unfettered by the burdens of history or preservation. Old buildings or resorts simply give way to the pressures of age or fashion and are remodeled, or, at the extreme, imploded, accompanied by fireworks and street-wide celebrations. Few remember, or perhaps even care, that the Italian-themed Venetian is on the site of the Sands – the Rat Pack's most famous haunt, while the SLS Las Vegas now stands on the foundations of the legendary Sahara.

Las Vegas is a city of reinvention. After the Rat Pack era of the 1960s, Sin City became a family-friendly destination, building theme parks and spectacular attractions designed with children in mind. This was a success throughout the 1990s, but the turn of the millennium brought a sea change. Families, it turns out, spend less time at the all-important gaming tables than singles or couples. Although

WORLD CAPITAL OF BOXING

Las Vegas probably has a better claim than any city to the title of 'the World's Capital of Boxing'. Vegas is often the promoters' choice as the venue for major title bouts, including world championships.

Sonny Liston, Muhammad Ali, Leon Spinks, Larry Holmes, Mike Spinks, George Foreman, and Evander Holyfield are just a few of the fighters to have won the heavyweight championship title in Las Vegas. After his retirement from the ring, Joe Louis stayed on and was popular as a greeter at Caesars Palace.

kid-friendly places such as Excalibur and Circus Circus still market to families, the emphasis has shifted to lure in as many high-spending adults as possible. Today's Las Vegas has world-class accommodations, five-star dining, and shopping that rivals any major city, adding to the town's reputation for all-night gambling, drinking, and adult-oriented diversions. Hotel-casinos have positioned themselves as complete resorts, offering day spas, evenings shows, and huge shopping malls – in addition to the gambling, golf courses, and showrooms, of course. Newer resorts, like Encore, the Palazzo, and the Cosmopolitan, aim to recapture the perceived glamor of the Rat Pack era. Always betting on growth, expansion, and the power of positive cash flow, Las Vegas continues to embrace new players: 2014 saw the opening of both the ultra-modern and opulent SLS Las Vegas and the epic High Roller observation wheel.

Gondoliers at the Venetian

REINVENTION

Such rapid change and reinvention results in what critics call a city without a soul. But for nearly 620,000 residents and some 41 million annual visitors, this characteristic – the city's instinct for the next big thing – makes Vegas the city of their dreams.

Outside the resort corridors, new suburban residential developments swallow the surrounding desert, edging to the bases of the mountain ranges east and west. Unlike the original American suburbs, new master-planned communities like Summerlin and Green Valley are thriving cities within themselves. New businesses spring up quickly, built into the plan and ready to serve an already-waiting community of clients. Driving through these areas feels like a ride through a movie set – the homes are sparkling and modern, the highways smooth and wide, and the landscaping young, fragile, and new.

LOCAL LAS VEGAS

Just a short way from the crowds and lights of the Strip and Fremont Street are quiet, ranch-style homes complete with swimming pools, tennis courts, horse corrals, and lush landscaping. The University of Nevada-Las Vegas mentors a student population of 28,000, although, like most people in Vegas, they commute through the endless gridlock that

Las Vegas show girls

now defines the streets. Before the recent rapid expansion, the city claimed to have more churches per capita than any other in the United States. Spiritual guidance was apparently a pressing need for dwellers who live in the shadow of temptation.

Although Las Vegas is still dominated by the gambling industry, non-gaming business flourishes here as well, thanks to a favorable tax structure. With the exception of Zappos.com, located into the old City Hall building Downtown, much of the non-gaming business is in suburban business parks and master-planned communities. This is part of a concerted effort to reinvent the metropolis with industrial and commercial centers across the valley. Credit-card companies and banks, mail order firms, health care subsidiaries, and software developers are all in the economic mix. These companies help Las Vegas diversify, as the national attitudes to gambling shift like the desert sands.

Las Vegas shows new cultural growth, too. Local theater is healthy, while a well-regarded public art museum and the Bellagio Gallery of Fine Art have brought world-class art collections to an eager public.

SPECTACULAR SPORTS

For sports fans, one of the attractions of this city in the desert is its easy access to athletic endeavors. Whether you watch a championship fight from a ring-side seat, catch auto-racer Jimmie Johnson roaring past the checkered flag at the Las Vegas Motor Speedway, or take active advantage of the golf, hot-air ballooning, tennis, hiking, or rock-climbing possibilities, nothing is ever far away. Nor are some of the most important wonders of the world, whether they are natural – like the Grand Canyon and Death Valley – or artificial, like the awe-inspiring Hoover Dam.

The grand facade of Caesars Palace

POWERFUL PRODUCTIONS

Las Vegas' shows – musical, magical, or theatrical – are among the best in the world, employing the finest from Hollywood to Broadway to design and build state-of-the-art performance arenas that encourage extravaganzas to reach new heights. Famous acts like Celine Dion, Cirque de Soleil, and Penn & Teller all have semi-permanent homes in Las Vegas, because the constantly changing audience makes it easier to produce a show-stopper than being constantly on the road.

GLITTERING MOMENTS

Las Vegas's transformations – from a watering hole to a gambling way-station to a desert retreat, and now, to an international resort city – have all been whistle-stops on the city's journey of evolution. This city, with its eyes firmly on the future, is never dull, and it continues to attract tourists who want to sample the glamorous Las Vegas lifestyle, if only for a few non-stop moments.

A BRIEF HISTORY

Humans have inhabited the Las Vegas Valley since at least 23,000 BC, when much of the area was covered by a pre-historic sea. The people of the time lived in nearby caves, hunting mammals that gathered at the shoreline. The landscape of the valley changed dramatically over the next 200 centuries. The glaciers melted, and the lake eventually evaporated. Scientists have used the fossilized remains of plants and animals to learn more about the region's past.

FIRST INHABITANTS

Around 3000 BC, Archaic people began to develop of a hunter-gatherer culture. At this time, the valley was geographically similar to how it appears today, although there were artesian springs bubbling to the surface that made the harsh desert landscape more hospitable. The springs fed a network of streams, draining through the Las Vegas Wash to the Colorado River. Surrounding the springs were desert oases, sprawls of grasses, trees, and wildlife. Many of the springs crossed the center of the modern Las Vegas metropolitan area.

For about 4,000 years, the Archaic people lived in the valley in a culture that displayed many of the hallmarks of early civilization. Change in the valley occurred halfway through the first millennium AD, with the arrival of the Anasazi people. More progressive than the Archaics, the Anasazi used agricultural techniques such as irrigation and crop rotation. The Anasazi reached a benchmark of advanced society – living in permanent shelters year-round,

Fish in the desert

Approximately 275 million years ago, the Mojave, Great Basin, and Sonoran deserts formed the floor of a great inland sea.

Native legacy

Native Americans inhabited the Las Vegas Valley for about 5,000 years. First came the so-called Archaics, then, around 300 BC the Anasazi, and more recently the Paiutes.

without the need to follow wildlife on their migration routes. Mysteriously, the Anasazi vanished from the Las Vegas valley around AD 1150; no one knows why the Anasazi left, or where they went, although there are many theories.

The valley was soon populated by another tribe, the Souther Paiutes. Unskilled in the agri-techniques of the Anasazi, the Paiutes were semi-nomadic until European settlers arrived and changed the cultural landscape of the valley.

FROM MAILMEN TO MORMONS

In the early 19th century, America's western territories were still largely unexplored. It was not until 1829 that Rafael Rivera, a Mexican scout, found a spring-fed valley and dubbed it *'Las Vegas'* – a Spanish name that leaves many modern visitors wondering exactly where 'the meadows' really are.

For 15 years, Las Vegas was used as a way-station on the Spanish Trail. In 1844, American explorer John C. Fremont parked his horses at Big Springs, and his report to the government resulted in a mail route leading past the spot on the way to California. This literally put Las Vegas on the map, and was one of the crucial turning points for the settlement. In 1855, Mormon leader Brigham Young responded to promising reports of this oasis by sending 30 missionary settlers to the valley; they eventually built a fort near today's downtown area. Surrounded by farmland hewn from the hard desert, this adobe fort was the center of Las

Vegas' development for 50 years. The missionaries struggled valiantly against the harsh desert, trying to both survive in the terrain and spread the Mormon faith, but pressures from arriving miners pushed the missionaries' plight beyond recovery. Their supplies scarce, their harvest meager, and their spirit broken, they abandoned the fort in 1858 and traveled north to Salt Lake City.

Although the local land was rich in silver, by 1865 most of the mining traffic through Las Vegas consisted of prospectors on their way to California or Northern Nevada in the quest for gold.

LAS VEGAS RANCH

One opportunist who stayed in Las Vegas was Octavius Decatur Gass. Having plenty of the pioneer spirit, Gass picked up where the Mormons left off, with ranching and farming. He took over the abandoned fort and 640 acres (260 hectares) surrounding it, naming it the Las Vegas Ranch. He expanded the ranch and irrigated the land to support crops and cattle. Gass became a Justice of the Peace and a territorial legislator, but despite his ambition, his success was short-lived. In the late 1870s, he defaulted on a

Explorer John C. Fremont

loan from rancher Archibald Stewart, and Stewart took the Las Vegas Ranch for his own. True to Wild-West stereotypes, Stewart was slain by a neighboring farmer, leaving the ranch to his strong-willed wife, Helen. Through 1905, Helen Stewart expanded the ranch to 2,000 acres (810 hectares), making quite a bit of money in the process.

OF TRACKS AND TRACTS

The arrival of the railroad changed Las Vegas forever, as it did for much of the United States. At the turn of the 19th century Los Angeles and Salt Lake City were among the burgeoning metropolises of the new American West. When the two cities were linked by rail, the Las Vegas Valley became an important link in the nationwide system of trains.

In 1903, officials of the San Pedro, Los Angeles and Salt Lake Railroad arrived in Las Vegas, eager to secure a right-of-way for their Los Angeles–Salt Lake connection. Las Vegas would serve as a major stopover for crew rest and train repairs. For this kind of infrastructure, the railroad needed land. As mapped, the track traveled directly through Helen Stewart's Las Vegas Ranch, so Stewart sold 99.5 percent of her ranch to the railroad. The remainder she returned to the Paiute tribe, and she also organized a school in the local Paiute colony.

The first casino

Mayme Stocker, the wife of a railroad man, was granted the first Las Vegas gambling license. She opened The Northern Club on Fremont Street in 1920.

The route between Los Angeles and Salt Lake City was completed in 1905; the tracks traveled right through the center of the Las Vegas Valley. On May 15, 1905, the railroad held a land sale – a milestone

Postcard of Union Pacific Station, 1941

in Las Vegas history. Standing at the depot at Main and Fremont streets, officials auctioned 1,200 lots, subdivided from 40 square blocks of desert scrub. Land speculators and locals alike were anxious for a part of the newest railroad boom town, and more than 80 percent of the lots were sold that afternoon.

Las Vegas was no longer just a small pioneer settlement. With rail service in place and 40 blocks of private property, it was ready to become a real town. Businesses sprang up, and wooden houses were erected to replace the tent city where many of the early settlers lived. One year after the auction, the population of Las Vegas swelled from fewer than 30 residents to more than 1,500 practically overnight.

DAM GOOD LUCK

From the beginning, Las Vegas served as a stopping point for travelers, first on the Spanish or Paiute Trail, then along the US Postal route. Now the railroad needed a way station, and Las Vegas was the place. By 1915, after 10 years of growth, the town had telephones, 24-hour electricity, and a growing population of more than 3,000 – many of whom worked in the railroad repair shop.

With growing competition in rail transport, Union Pacific bought the Los Angeles–Salt Lake line. Union Pacific then consolidated its operations, eliminating the Las Vegas repair facility. Las Vegas had been incorporated into Nevada's new Clark County in 1909, when the legislature also outlawed gambling. These circumstances threatened to relegate Las Vegas to the status of a small desert community struggling to support its 3,000 residents. But the Southwest's growing need for water, combined with fortuitous proximity to the Colorado River, would give Las Vegas a second chance of prosperity. Construction on the Hoover Dam (originally

Jake Freedman, owner of the Sands, at the roulette table

called the Boulder Dam, and later renamed for the president who authorized it) began in 1931, in a canyon 45 miles (72km) southeast of Las Vegas.

The magnificent bridge over the Hoover Dam

Bringing $165 million to the region's economy, the Hoover Dam prevented Las Vegas from drying up, both financially and literally, during the dust bowl years of the Great Depression. The project brought jobs to the area and also created Lake Mead, the massive reservoir that provides the water for the whole of southern Nevada.

PUBLIC RELATIONS

The construction of the Hoover Dam wasn't Las Vegas' sole savior, however. The state legislature helped too, legalizing gambling in 1931 and securing the future of the town. The hordes of people who attended the dam's 1935 dedication set the city's now-formidable public relations machine into action. They went to work on what has become one of the lengthiest tourism campaigns ever attempted. The city soon established itself as a Wild-West town with an 'anything goes' attitude. Vices outlawed or heavily controlled elsewhere were legal here, at any hour of any day or night. So began Las Vegas's reputation as an adult theme park.

Further fuel for the valley's economy came with World War II. The Las Vegas Aerial Gunnery School (now Nellis Air Force Base), the Nevada Test Site (for nuclear weapons testing), and Basic Magnesium Plant in nearby Henderson (which supplied the US War Department with magnesium for weapons and engines), grew from America's war effort. By 1945, the population had grown to almost 20,000, with workers and servicemen moving in to a growing city.

GAMBLING AND THE RAT PACK

Gaming thrived in downtown Las Vegas in the 1930s and early 1940s, and casinos began to develop on the stretch of the old Los Angeles Highway now known as the Strip; El Rancho Vegas was the first, opening in 1941. Money for the new casinos came largely from the Teamsters Union, the public face of organized crime. The Teamsters funded the Stardust and other casino operations; the unions' total investment in Las Vegas was shown to exceed $238 million. Law enforcement investigations, beginning with

BUGSY'S FLAMINGO

In 1946, Benjamin 'Bugsy' Siegel opened the Flamingo, an opulent resort on the southern end of the LA Highway. His vision combined Hollywood flair with money from organized crime. While he might have had a good idea, Siegel had no construction or resort management experience, and his ineptitude caused the project's costs to spiral out of control. Rumor has it that thieves would steal building supplies from the construction site at night, and sell the same materials back to Siegel the next day (sometimes several times). Although the $6 million resort opened on December 6 1946, the Flamingo failed to earn the staggering amounts of cash needed to pay off the debts to the mob. The Mafia bosses who financed the Flamingo were convinced that Siegel was skimming money from the resort, and they had him killed in June 1947.

the hearings of Tennessee Senator Estes Kefauver in 1950, took until the late 1960s to make a serious impact on the influence of organized crime in the Las Vegas gaming business.

From the mid-1940s to the mid-1960s, emerging stars came to Las Vegas with dreams of making it big: Frank Sinatra, Wayne Newton, and Louis Prima

Former Vegas resident Howard Hughes

among them. The Rat Pack – originally Frank Sinatra, Dean Martin, Sammy Davis Jr, Peter Lawford, and Joey Bishop, made legendary appearances at the Sands in January 1960, including filming the original *Ocean's 11*. To capitalize on the increasing popularity, more casinos emerged along the Strip, including the Desert Inn, Sahara, Sands, and Riviera.

NEW LEGITIMACY

In the 1960s, organized crime met a formidable rival for control of Las Vegas: corporate cash. First came the arrival of billionaire Howard Hughes in 1966. As a recluse and an invalid, Hughes was carried on a stretcher to the Desert Inn's penthouse. Six weeks later he was politely asked – then firmly instructed – to vacate the suite for the high rollers who had previously booked it. Instead of packing his bags, Hughes bought the Desert Inn and fired the management. During his three-year residence, he never once allowed cleaners into his suite, and he saw no-one face to face except for his bodyguards. Hughes didn't limit his purchases to the Desert Inn, his $300 million Las Vegas buying spree took in many properties along the Strip, plus plots of land from the Strip to the mountains.

Hughes' influence would have beneficial repercussions, both immediate and lasting. Because of the legitimacy Hughes conferred on the city with his investments, established companies such as Hilton Hotels bought into the gaming business, and their influence drew a line in the desert sand between lawful operations and mob casinos, where illegal skimming of profits was rife. That, and the formation of the Nevada Gaming Control Board, helped turn the tide against mob influence in the city.

LAS VEGAS WITH A VISION

The legitimization of gambling led to disorganization and reassessment. Competition forced casino operators to

The Luxor resort

look at their business models and markets. Leading the way was Steve Wynn, a Vegas resident and owner of the Golden Nugget casino. In the mid-1980s, Wynn began to reinvigorate the Strip.

Wynn bought several key properties – the Silver Slipper and Castaways among them – and demolished the structures to make way for a new kind of resort: the Mirage. It was an instant success. Wynn's demolition of existing properties started a trend that led to many more implosions. The Dunes was replaced by Bellagio, Aladdin by the new Aladdin, and the Sands made way for the Venetian. Wynn's casinos have also set new standards of fantasy – Excalibur, the MGM Grand, the Luxor, and New York-New York all followed Mirage's lead during the 1990s, offering themed environments and family attractions.

Collecting casions

Howard Hughes stayed in Las Vegas for almost three years. In that time he bought the Desert Inn, Landmark, Frontier, Silver Slipper, and Sands casinos, three parcels of land on the Strip, an airline, and a television station. According to legend he bought the TV station just so he could choose the late-night films that were aired.

THE MODERN ERA

By the middle of the 1990s, the new approach brought a backlash; visitors found the Las Vegas experience was becoming mediocre. In response, new resorts started to offer attractions and amenities modeled after top worldwide resorts, including luxurious spas and fabulous pools, signature restaurants, and exclusive boutiques.

Some of these resorts – such as Wynn, Mandalay Bay, the Venetian, Bellagio, the Cosmopolitan, and the SLS Las Vegas – now market themselves squarely at the luxury

The Vdara Hotel and Spa

travel market. Guests at these resorts expect the best; amenities include five-star dining, personal attention, and world-class art exhibits. These high-end accommodations with their glittering clientele have raised expectations above even the glamorous era of the Rat Pack.

CITY OF THE FUTURE

Las Vegas continues to change. CityCenter – which includes Aria, Vdara, Mandarin Oriental, and the Crystals shopping, dining, and entertainment complex, opened in 2010 and is now a city within the city. The LINQ Promenade is another pedestrian-only district, which made its debut in 2014. New upscale resorts in Summerlin and Lake Las Vegas cater to locals. Most of the remaining Rat-Pack-era Strip hotels have been demolished to make way for big condominium projects. In 2015, Sin City said farewell to the legendary Riviera. Still, recent projections for Las Vegas predict challenges; revenues need to rise to sustain investments, and a shortage of power – essential to air-condition and spotlight this neon nirvana in the desert – is an on-going concern.

The future of Las Vegas is sure to be based on the pioneering spirit that built the city from a few springs in the desert to the fantasy that it is today.

HISTORICAL LANDMARKS

1150 Paiute Indians inhabit Las Vegas Valley, replacing the Anasazi.

1829 Scout Raphael Rivera discovers springs in the desert and names the land 'Las Vegas,' which is Spanish for 'the meadows.'

1844 Explorer John C. Fremont camps at Las Vegas Springs, on a site that later bears his name, Fremont Street.

1848 The US acquires the region after winning the Mexican War.

1855 Mormon settlers build an adobe fort to protect the mail route.

1905 The San Pedro, Los Angeles & Salt Lake Railroad makes an inaugural run and auctions lots in a new town called Las Vegas.

1931 Construction of the Hoover Dam commences.

1931 Gambling is legalized in Nevada.

1941 El Rancho Vegas is the first casino to open on the stretch of Los Angeles Highway that later became known as the Strip.

1946 Benjamin 'Bugsy' Siegel, a member of the Meyer Lansky crime organization, opens the Flamingo Hotel.

1960 The Rat Pack shows, with Frank Sinatra, Sammy Davis Jr, Dean Martin, Peter Lawford, and Joey Bishop, sell out the Sands.

1966 Howard Hughes' arrival at the Desert Inn heralds the new corporate era of Las Vegas gaming.

1975 Nevada gaming revenues top $1 billion.

1980 Las Vegas (population 164,674) celebrates its 75th birthday.

1989 Steve Wynn opens the Mirage casino with 3,039 rooms.

1995 The Fremont Street Experience opens. A monorail connects the MGM Grand and Bally's.

1999 Mandalay Bay, New York-New York, and Paris Las Vegas open.

2001 The famous Desert Inn is imploded.

2004 Monorail extension runs the length of the Strip.

2005 The luxurious Wynn Las Vegas opens on the Strip.

2006 The Aladdin resort rebrands itself as Planet Hollywood.

2010 City Center opens. Metropolitan-area population nears 2 million.

2014 SLS Hotel and Casino Las Vegas debuts on the site of the legendary Sahara resort. The High Roller at LINQ opens.

2015 The iconic Riviera with its live topless shows closes down.

WHERE TO GO

Since Bugsy Siegel's Flamingo Hotel first opened in 1946, nothing in the world has rivaled the Las Vegas Strip's audacity or the casinos' desire to outdo one another. This 3.5-mile (5.5-km) section of the old Los Angeles Highway is both famous and notorious for its extravagant recreation. Stretching from the Mandalay Bay resort in the south to the Stratosphere Tower to the north, this one road has evoked more melodrama and mythology than the rest of the city combined.

Miles of neon tubing and millions of dazzling fiber-optic lights illuminate every hour of darkness year-round, while casinos leave the doors to their air-conditioned interiors wide open, even while the summer sun beats down at 115°F (46°C). Miles of food is prepared, cooked and put out every day for the all-you-can-eat buffets, even though only a small portion of it is ever consumed. The excess is staggering, but visitors come to Las Vegas to play and partake in the spectacle.

GLITTERING PLAYGROUND

A cornucopia of resorts, stores, restaurants, and casinos line both sides of the thoroughfare, tantalizing onlookers. Dozens of the world's largest hotels are congregated directly around the action, simply because the hotels *are* the major attractions. Some of these mega-resorts revel in the clichés of the past, while others offer a chic opulence that borders on the unreal. Roman palaces, the Eiffel Tower, the pyramids of ancient Egypt, and the jungles of Polynesia all await those with a yearning to indulge in the extravagance – and a bank account to withstand the trip.

Welcome to Las Vegas!

THE SOUTH END OF THE STRIP

At the southernmost end of the glittering Strip is the **Mandalay Bay Resort and Casino ❶** (www.mandalaybay. com). The $950-million behemoth is home to the luxurious suites at Delano Las Vegas and the **Shark Reef Aquarium** (www.sharkreef.com) with over 2,000 animals and a shark tunnel. Also featured are a House of Blues restaurant and club, a 12,000-seat arena, a convention center, and spa. Mandalay's excellent restaurants include RM Seafood, Fleur (from Hubert Keller), and Wolfgang Puck's Trattoria del Lupo.

Mandalay also offers one of Las Vegas's only nongaming resorts: the **Four Seasons Hotel Las Vegas** (www.four seasons.com/lasvegas). A total of 424 ultra-luxury rooms and suites occupy floors 35 to 39 of the main Mandalay tower, and are reachable via private elevator. The Four Seasons has a separate lobby, as well as two of its own restaurants, a health spa, meeting rooms, and a private pool set in a lush garden. If you prefer more of a scene, there's a doorway to the Mandalay pool from there.

Next up along the Strip is the mighty black peak of the **Luxor Hotel and Casino ❷** (www.luxor.com), 30 stories

LOST CIVILIZATION

It was not easy to tone down the ancient-Egyptian theme in a hotel shaped like a giant pyramid, but that's exactly what the Luxor has done. The resort has declared a new Art Deco ambiance (a style that incorporates some Egyptian elements). The bazaar-themed gaming area has been supplanted by chic clubs and restaurants. Some of the guest rooms have been redone with upscale modern flare. But there is still plenty of Egypt to be found, from the Sphinx out front to the Pyramid itself; the details have just been made a bit more sleek and subtle.

of tinted glass and steel topped with a night-defiant shaft of light, visible by air from Los Angeles. Encompassing the world's largest atrium, the pyramid (and its two adjoining towers) houses more than 4,400 rooms and a stunningly huge casino. There are other attractions worth noting, including the Nurture Spa, Savile Row lounge, the LAX nightclub, and wildly energetic and entertaining performances from the Blue Man Group. One of the biggest thrills for guests of the hotel is the ride up to

The Excalibur

the guest rooms on the inclinator, an elevator that moves up and sideways at the same time. There are four sets of inclinators, all located at the pyramid's corners, which can be inconvenient if your room is located in the center of the sloping walls.

EXCALIBUR

One of the oldest themed resorts, the **Excalibur Hotel and Casino** (www.excalibur.com) is a Medieval Faire aimed squarely at families and travelers on a budget. This is evident in the execution – though in no way shoddy, the overall experience is cheap and cheerful. For a brief period, the Excalibur was the largest hotel in the world, though its 3,981 rooms were soon surpassed by the MGM Grand. One of its attractions is the rowdy Tournament of Kings, a re-creation of a Middle Ages jousting tournament, and one of the few dinner shows left in Las Vegas. The casino caters mostly to minimum betters, with (occasional) $5 blackjack tables and penny slot machines. The resort, like most of Las Vegas, is definitely seen at its best at night – viewed from the Strip, the brightly illuminated spires and battlements are a fine sight.

TROPICANA

The smallest and oldest of the four resorts at the busy intersection of Las Vegas Boulevard and Tropicana Avenue, the **Tropicana Las Vegas Hotel and Casino** ❸ (www.troplv.com), decorated in Island style, has some of the largest guest rooms on the Strip. Outside, the all-white Nikki Beach Club and pool complex evokes South Beach chic, and attracts only the most beautiful sunbathers. The casino is also home to the Laugh Factory comedy club.

MGM GRAND

Across the Strip, the **MGM Grand Hotel and Casino** (www.mgm grand.com) is so massive – the casino floor is the size of four American football fields – that most visitors become disoriented as they wander the resort. The theming here is subtle, and

Nikki Beach Club at at the Tropicana

incorporates MGM's most famous movies. How big is big? Try 5,044 guest rooms spread across 114 acres (46 hectares), 22 places to eat (including establishments by Wolfgang Puck, Joël Robuchon, Emeril Lagasse, and Michael Mina), an elaborate 6.5-acre (3-hectare) pool complex, a spa and tennis facility, three arenas, including the enormous Grand Garden Arena (site of some of Vegas' biggest rock concerts), a comedy club, and the Hakkasan nightclub. There are four gaming areas, and minimum bets ranging from $10 to $500, as well as nearly 4,000 slot machines, a poker room and a lively (though small) sports book. High rollers may be offered

Optical illusions

Las Vegas may be the only place on Earth where architects work to make buildings seem smaller than they are.

accommodations in one of 30 private villas at the Mansion; for apartment-style accommodations, try the Signature at MGM Grand, which boasts 1,728 suites.

NEW YORK-NEW YORK

Taking theme hotels to a new level, the **New York-New York Las Vegas Hotel and Casino** (www.nynyhotelcasino.com) actually spawned lawsuits by several Manhattan architects. Its dozen towers are uncanny, one-third-size replicas of famous New York skyscrapers, including the Empire State Building, New York Public Library, and Chrysler Building. Inside, the detailed illusion continues with cartoon quality, such as the fake subway station complete with graffiti and a food court designed to look like Greenwich Village. The casino, which has high ceilings (a rarity in Vegas), was redesigned in 2010 to evoke the Art Deco era; the Center Bar is a great place to sip old-school martinis. Guestrooms have names like Park Avenue Deluxe, while shopping areas are called Soho Village and Grand Central. The **Big Apple Coaster** (daily 10.30am–midnight) is worth the wait.

MONTE CARLO

The **Monte Carlo Resort and Casino** (www.montecarlo.com) evokes a classic Las Vegas atmosphere, remarkably accessible to any traveler. Striking in its elegant European theme, this resort has an understated style that is rare in modern Las Vegas. In homage to tradition, the resort offers a wide range of gaming, dining, retail, and spa amenities. Though it looks like a haven for high rollers, minimum bets are actually quite modest, starting at $5; they even have penny slots.

In 2016, the area between the New York-New York and the Monte Carlo Resort will see the opening of the **Las Vegas Arena** (www.arenalasvegas.com), a 20,000-seat venue for major entertainment and sports events.

THE CENTER STRIP

CITYCENTER

The ultra-modern, $9.2-billion **CityCenter** ❹ (www2.citycenter.com) marks the official half-way point of the Strip. The sleek buildings – hotels, apartments, and retail – comprise the largest privately financed development in the US. It's truly a sight to behold. Anchoring the complex is **Aria Resort and Casino**, one of three hotels and the only one with a casino (as well as a dozen celebrated restaurants). All 4,004 rooms feature floor-to-ceiling windows

The Brooklyn Bridge at New York-New York

The casino at The Cosmopolitan

and a touchpad from which guests can open the curtains, turn off the lights, and control the music. Next door, **Vdara Hotel and Spa** offers apartment-style suites. Closer to the Strip, the **Mandarin Oriental Las Vegas** redefines luxury with guest rooms that spare no expense. The **Mandarin Bar**, on the 23rd floor, also offers some of the most commanding views in town.

Completing the complex is the **Crystals** shopping, dining, and entertainment center (www.theshopsatcrystals.com), a mall of high-end shops and restaurants. This facility – all of CityCenter, for that matter – also features an impressive display of public art.

THE COSMOPOLITAN

Hipsters are right at home at **The Cosmopolitan of Las Vegas** ❺ (www.cosmopolitanlasvegas.com), located between CityCenter and Bellagio. The star of the show: **The Chandelier**, a three-story bar designed to make cocktail-drinkers feel as if they're sitting inside a chandelier. Upstairs, most of the 2,995 rooms boast open-air balconies, a Vegas first. What's more, mini-bars feature Yoo-Hoo, a chocolate milk-like beverage many Americans had in primary school. Restaurant offerings are expansive, and include the high-end Greek eatery Estiatorio Milos. Nightclub and 'dayclub' options always draw a crowd, too, and the Cosmo's pool offers one of the best see-and-be-seen vibes on the Strip.

PLANET HOLLYWOOD

Across the street from CityCenter is the **Planet Hollywood Resort and Casino** ❻ (www.caesars.com/planet-hollywood), formerly the Aladdin. The original 1960s Aladdin played host to the 1967 wedding of Elvis and Priscilla Presley. It was reopened in 1976 after a total renovation and was owned for a time by Vegas legend Wayne Newton. The hotel was imploded in 1998, and a new 21st-century version was opened in August 2000. In 2007, the Aladdin re-emerged as Planet Hollywood, complete with celebrity-inspired decor. Floor-to-ceiling Swarovski crystal chandeliers adorn the lobby, while the swimming pool and spa overlook the Strip. Adjoining the resort is the spectacular **Miracle Mile Shops** (www.miraclemileshopslv. com) promenade, with a distinctive array of 170 stores, 15 restaurants, an indoor waterfall, and the AXIS auditorium, the venue for such megastars as Britney Spears and Jennifer Lopez.

Paris Las Vegas

PARIS AND BALLY'S

The 2,900-room **Paris Las Vegas** ❼ (www.caesars.com/paris-las-vegas) took the theme concept to new levels with a massive property modeled after the Hôtel de Ville in Paris. The property is a Vegas-style homage to the city of romance, complete with the Arc de Triomphe.

Patrons can see the bright city lights from the top of the one-half scale Eiffel Tower, go shopping on the Rue de la Paix, or dine in one of several Parisian-inspired eateries, including a restaurant in the tower itself. Faux cobblestone walkways lead to other landmark replicas, among them the Paris Opera House and the Louvre. Be prepared for high stakes in the gilded casino, however, where gaming opportunities include more than 2,000 slot machines.

One of the old guard of Las Vegas resorts, **Bally's Las Vegas** has eschewed major transformation over the years, with the exception of its Jubilee Tower, which was thoroughly renovated in 2014. Despite the futuristic light-and-water show out front, Bally's is an exercise in classic Las Vegas style. Inside, all is comfortable and inviting, with dark colors and chandeliers hanging above the casino floor. Because table minimums usually are low, this is a great place to learn

The lobby of the Bellagio

how to play games such as poker, blackjack, craps, and roulette. The showroom features the adults-only show, Donn Arden's *Jubilee!,* and an entertaining parady of the novel *Fifty Shades of Grey.* For a real splurge, try the Sterling Brunch.

Glass ceiling

The iridescent glass sculpture over the lobby at Bellagio cost more than $10 million. It was designed and created by Dale Chihuly, the first American to be accepted by the Italian glassmakers of Murano.

BELLAGIO

One of the most lavish resorts in Las Vegas is the **Bellagio ❽**, a stunning replica of an Italian villa that boasted an equally stunning price tag at the time: $1.6 billion. Gaming rooms offer an unlikely quiet elegance, while the **Bellagio Gallery of Fine Art** (daily 10am–8pm) hosts traveling exhibitions. The dining is unparalleled (try Picasso), as are the luxurious accommodations. The conservatory features a lavish display of flowers, which changes with the seasons. One of the highlights of Vegas is the dazzling choreographed water show in the small lake fronting the resort. Another highlight is Cirque du Soleil's remarkable aquatic show, *O* (note that tickets don't come cheap and are booked far in advance). Shopping in the hall of retail fame that is Via Bellagio is for big spenders. Tiffany and Prada both have stores here, and if you can't afford the price tags, it's always fun to window shop.

THE NORTH END OF THE STRIP

With a handful of construction and renovation projects, the North Strip continues to evolve. Occupying a powerful corner of the famed boulevard, the former Bill's Gamblin' Hall and Saloon reopened in 2014 as the **Cromwell Las Vegas** (www.thecromwell.com), while the $4-billion Chinese-themed

Stellar sideshows

The Mirage's volcano and the fountains of Bellagio draw crowds that stop traffic. This is one reason the LVPD are so tough on jay-walkers.

Resorts World (www.rwlas vegas.com) is expected to open in 2018.

The venerable **Flamingo Las Vegas** (www.caesars. com/flamingo-las-vegas) retains Bugsy Siegel's original theme of a desert oasis with a lushly restful tropical pool and garden area complete with swans, ducks, penguins, and flamingos. Little of the older hotel remains, though Siegel is commemorated by a small plaque near the wedding garden. Amenities include seven restaurants, three bars, two pools, a spa, a beauty salon, and several boutiques. Most gaming tables offer low minimum bets, and slot junkies have a choice of more than 2,000 machines.

CAESARS PALACE

A standard-setter since its 1968 opening, **Caesars Palace** ❾ (www.caesars.com/caesars-palace) is one of the few old-timers to keep pace with modern Las Vegas, perhaps because its ancient Rome theme is still popular (genuine marble never seems to go out of style). Here, elegance seems within anyone's reach, though having lots of money certainly helps. The casino is a high-roller's heaven with lofty limits at many tables. Sports fans will enjoy the lively environment at the Sports Book, which boasts three of the biggest big screens in town. Spa lovers swear by Qua Baths & Spa, and the Garden of the Gods Pool Oasis features eight pools (including one with swim-up blackjack). The adjacent Colosseum hosts Celine Dion's shows (see page 86). The popular and respected **Forum Shops** offers a fabulous spread of shopping, as well as dining for any budget.

LINQ AND HARRAH'S

Recognizable by its blue-neon tinted pagoda, the sprawling **LINQ** (www.caesars.com/linq), formerly known as Imperial Palace Las Vegas, houses 2,640 rooms, numerous restaurants, and a 75,000-sq-ft (6,975-sq-m) casino. Aside from the gaming room, the most popular draw here is the **High Roller**, the world's tallest observation wheel with 28 glass-enclosed cabins located on the Linq Promenade, a pedestrian-only dining, retail and entertainment district. **The Auto Collections** (http://autocollections.com; daily 10am–6pm) boasts more than 300 vehicles and bills itself as the world's largest classic car museum. Check out Marilyn Monroe's convertible.

Harrah's Las Vegas (www.caesars.com/harrahs-las-vegas) is a profusion of bright colors, fiber-optic fireworks, tropical palm trees, and huge murals of international fêtes. It's a sizable establishment, with more than 2,600 guest rooms and an

Forum shops at Caesar's Palace

enormous gaming area. Seven restaurants offer a welcome respite from the glitz, but the real fun is in the Improv comedy club, which showcases three new comedians each week.

VENETIAN AND PALAZZO

The Venetian Resort Hotel Casino ❿ (www.venetian.com) evokes Renaissance Venice with dramatic replicas of the Doge's Palace, Campanile, and canals with gondolas and serenading gondoliers. It's an elegant, upscale resort with the renowned Canyon Ranch Spa on its premises, and enough marble-and-stone flooring to cover a dozen football fields. A real centerpiece of the complex is the **Grand Canal Shoppes**, a collection of beautiful stores and restaurants. All of the property's 4,027 rooms are suites.

The **Palazzo Resort Hotel Casino** ⓫ (www.palazzo.com), adjacent to the Venetian and under the same ownership, essentially offers more of the same: an additional 3,068 suites, more high-end restaurants, and additional luxury shopping. One major difference: Lagasse's Stadium, a sports book with a sports bar and a restaurant operated by celebrity chef Emeril Lagasse.

THE MIRAGE

The pioneer of modern themed resorts, **The Mirage** ⓬ (www.mirage.com) shows its age when compared to the newer resorts. Still, it is attractive to both high- and low-rollers, owing to a lush environment and stylish accommodations. The pool area is particularly pleasant. On the casino floor, the Revolution Lounge – crafted in tandem with the Beatles theme from

Viva Venezia

Gondoliers were recruited from the ranks of boatmen in Venice, Italy, to ply the Venetian's Grand Canal at the casino's opening.

The Mirage

the on-site Cirque du Soleil show – is a great place to meet friends for drinks. Elsewhere on site, 15 restaurants and cafés feed the hungry masses with everything from buffet fare to gourmet cuisine. Near the check-in desk is an incredible and mesmerizing aquarium.

Fronting the hotel is the famous Mirage volcano, redesigned in 2009 with help from Grateful Dead drummer Mickey Hart. Another big attraction is **Siegfried and Roy's Secret Garden and Dolphin Habitat** (www.miragehabitat.com), roamed by Siegfried and Roy's famous white tigers. The duo of blond magicians put their wands away for the last time in 2003, when, on Roy Horn's birthday, October 3, the illusionist was savagely mauled during the show by one of the tigers. A larger-than-life statue of the duo stands in a plaza in front of the hotel.

TREASURE ISLAND (TI)
Treasure Island Hotel and Casino (www.treasureisland.com) has distanced itself from its original pirate theme.

The popular *Sirens of TI* show featuring sexy sirens and a renegade group of pirate is gone too. The resort now hosts *Mystère*, the classic Cirque du Soleil show which premiered in 1993 and celebrated its 10,000th show 21 years later.

WYNN AND ENCORE

The Desert Inn, a Las Vegas classic, was imploded in 2001 to make way for entrepreneur Steve Wynn's $1.6 billion fantasy, **Wynn Las Vegas** ⑬ (www.wynnlasvegas.com). Dominating this part of the Strip, the sweeping, shiny black resort is also home to the tycoon's fabulous art collection, which is distributed throughout the hotel's common areas. The hotel also houses an indoor mountain, backed by a huge curtain waterfall that spills into a three-acre indoor lake. Behind the hotel lies an 18-hole championship golf course designed by Tom Fazio for the exclusive use

The Encore at Wynn Las Vegas

of Wynn's guests, while the Wynn Esplanade features luxury labels including Dior, Chanel, Manolo Blahnik, and Alexander McQueen.

Next door, at the $2.3-billion **Encore** ⑭, Wynn has taken his signature elegance a step further, offering up 2,034 all-suite accommodations and a casino floor with – gasp! – windows that let in natural light. Also of note here is the Encore Beach Club, a standalone pool complex with cabanas, open-air gaming, and a party atmosphere that thumps well into the morning four days a week.

The Stratosphere

CIRCUS CIRCUS AND SLS LAS VEGAS

The first of the family-friendly low-roller casinos over two decades ago, **Circus Circus Las Vegas Hotel and Casino** (www.circuscircus.com) shows signs of fatigue, despite several renovations. However, families still appreciate the free circus acts every half-hour from 11am to midnight, the carnival games, arcade, and giant indoor amusement park, **Adventuredome**. The huge casino area is separated into three areas, connected by walkways and a monorail. Compared to the rest of the Strip, Circus Circus is a throwback that attracts low-rollers looking for cheap thrills.

When it opened in 1955, the nine-story **Riviera Hotel and Casino** was the Strip's first high-rise and famous for its live topless shows. Some of the showgirls have been immortalized by a bronze sculpture of their rear-ends, now on display at Planet Hollywood.

The glamorous **SLS Las Vegas** (http://slslasvegas.com), on the site of the legendary Sahara resort, has 1,1620 opulent rooms devised by renowned designer Philippe Starck and a 60,000-sq-ft (5,674-sq-m) casino, although the hotel's award-winning restaurants and premier nightclubs are what draw the crowds here.

THE STRATOSPHERE

The **Stratosphere Casino, Hotel and Tower** ❶ (www.stratospherehotel.com) struggles against the challenges of location – too far north for the Strip, too far south for Downtown. The hotel's centerpiece is the 1,149-ft (350-m) tower, which includes a 109th-floor observation deck (one of the highest in the US), an 83rd-floor revolving restaurant with reasonable food, and four thrill rides (the **Big Shot** and **X-Scream** are truly frightening).

Along with the requisite gaming area – which is well thought of for its loose slots and low-limit tables – are more than 14 restaurants and more than 40 stores. Lovers with stars in their eyes can get hitched in the **Chapel in the Clouds**, which hovers 100 stories above the Strip.

Light Fantastic

More than 12.5 million LEDs and a 550,000-watt sound system deliver the dazzling spectacle of Viva Vision. The moving picture show features jet fighters, exotic birds, and dancing girls.

DOWNTOWN

While the wonders of the Strip eclipsed Downtown early in the city's history, the area still has much to offer visitors. Both the city's oldest casino (El Cortez) and its oldest hotel (the Golden Gate, where Las Vegas's first

telephone was installed) are located Downtown, as are numerous other properties, including magnate Steve Wynn's first, the Golden Nugget.

Until recently, Fremont Street was Las Vegas's civic gathering spot, home to holiday parades and the Wild-West-themed Helldorado festival. Over time, the shopping moved to the suburbs and the attorneys moved to high-rise offices just outside the gaming area. In the face of stagnating revenues, local Downtown government and business owners have tried

Bustling Downtown

to explore ways to increase traffic to the famed district. One lure has been the opening of **Las Vegas Premium Outlets**, just off Interstate 15 and Charleston Boulevard.

FREMONT STREET EXPERIENCE

The incredible **Fremont Street Experience** ❻ (http://vegas experience.com) is one of the area's greatest draws. The combined project of casino owners and the city, this part of Fremont Street, between Las Vegas Boulevard and Main Street, was closed to automobile traffic and landscaped into a pedestrian mall at an original cost of $70 million. The Experience's most impressive feature is the 90-ft (2.75-m) high vaulted canopy that plays host to **Viva Vision**, a 6-minute long audio-visual show, said to be the world's

Fremont Street Experience

largest (shows every hour, starting at dusk, until midnight or 1am in summer). Between the hourly light shows, live musicians offer free entertainment on two stages. Apart from making the area friendlier, the Experience also cleaned up the Downtown city blocks – at least the part under its influence. There's also a zipline that allows you to soar above the crowds on Fremont Street at up to 30 mph (48kph).

The Experience was later joined by a non-gaming entertainment complex called **Neonopolis**. The $99-million complex features the **Southern Nevada Museum of Fine Art** (www.snmfa.com; Wed–Sat noon–5pm), restaurants, shopping and underground parking. It is part of the **Fremont East Entertainment District**, refurbished with an array of vintage neon signs.

Fremont is a throwback to the old days of Las Vegas gaming. House gambling rules are generally more flexible, allowing for both lower minimum bets and higher limits.

Additionally, there is a certain rough quality to Downtown, an experience different from the glittering Strip resorts. Do not mistake this edginess for danger; the Fremont Street Experience has done quite a bit to improve the safety of the area, sometimes drawing the ire of civil rights and free speech activists. Note that the darker reaches of central Downtown are still considered unsafe for tourists.

MAIN STREET STATION AND THE PLAZA

Main Street Station Casino, Brewery and Hotel (www.main streetcasino.com) is perhaps Downtown's best-kept secret. Just north of the Fremont Street Experience, this Victorian-styled casino fulfills the promise of the exterior architecture and gas-fired street lamps with a detailed interior filled with antiques. Unlike other casinos, Main Street showcases genuine articles; a carved Scottish fireplace and Teddy Roosevelt's Pullman car among them. The restaurants here – an all-you-can-eat buffet and brewpub – aren't too bad, either.

The neon **Plaza Hotel and Casino** (www.plazahotelcasino. com) is located at the west end of the Fremont Street Experience canopy. For decades the hotel had a dark, smoky, 1970s feel; renovations in 2010 modernized a good bit of the period kitsch. Today, with just over 1,000 rooms and a 75,000-sq-ft (6,975-sq-m) gaming area that includes penny slots, the Plaza attracts an interesting mix of friendly gamblers and seniors. The showroom offers campy, adult-oriented revues.

Will lady luck shine on you?

FREMONT STREET CASINOS

The **Las Vegas Club Hotel and Casino** (www.lasvegasclub casino.com), one of the oldest casinos in Las Vegas, marks the beginning of the Fremont Experience canopy. Explore 40,000 sq ft (3,720 sq m) of gaming with some of the most liberal house rules in town. The modest theming here features a widely dispersed exhibition of sports memorabilia, as well as card dealers dressed in jersey-like uniforms. The hotel tower was added in 1980 and features 410 affordable, comfortable rooms. There are also three casual restaurants and a food court.

The San Francisco-styled **Golden Gate Hotel and Casino** (www.goldengatecasino.com) has stood at One Fremont Street since 1906. The charming operation is the city's oldest hotel, the home of its first telephone, and the original purveyor of the classic shrimp cocktail. Its 106 small but pleasant rooms with plaster walls and mahogany doors hark back

The Golden Nugget's shimmering facade

to another era, and its coffee shop is an original, if not too classy, Downtown experience. Piano players entertain with infectious ragtime.

The only prominent Downtown hotel-casino without a multicolored neon sign (though its facade is completely covered with small golden lightbulbs), the 1946 **Golden Nugget Hotel** (www.goldennugget.com), was remodeled as Steve Wynn's *Slot machines at Paris Las Vegas* first hotel project in 1987.

Metropolitan elegance supersedes the surrounding glitz. Guests, greeted by uniformed doormen, enter a gilded lobby full of marble and crystal. The Rush Tower, the hotel's newest addition, has rooms that are modern and chic. The star of the show at the Nugget, however, is the pool, a $30 million extravaganza known as the Tank. Soak up the sun from a rented cabana or speed down the three-story slide that goes right through a shark tank.

A blinding neon landmark since 1966, the **Four Queens Hotel and Casino** (www.fourqueens.com) attracts older guests, many of whom are repeat customers. Low table minimums and a giant slot machine draws players to the 60,000-sq-ft (5,580-sq-m) casino. The 700 rooms of earth-tone decor are pleasant and affordable. Its four restaurants include Hugo's Cellar, an always-busy classic Las Vegas gourmet room with a winning wine list.

Formerly known as Fitzgerald's, the **D Casino and Hotel** (www.thed.com) is the Las Vegas low-rollers' gaming haven.

Once the tallest building in Nevada at 34 stories, its 638 rooms offer terrific views of the city and the mountains. Accommodations are of the national chain-hotel variety, and priced accordingly (ie not expensive), as are several restaurants and bars.

Founded by gambler Benny Binion, **Binion's Gambling Hall** ⑰ (www.binions.com) may be the most traditional, old-school gaming joint left in town. The casino has shut down its hotel, but still has some of the highest betting limits in Vegas. Billed as 'the Place that Made Poker Famous,' the family-run Binion's hosted the World Series of Poker for many action-packed years, until Becky Binion sold the casino in 2004. The Binion family come from Texas ranching stock, so premium beef is on offer in the coffeeshop and the Top of Binion's Steak House.

SLOT MACHINES

Slot machines generate more than two-thirds of Nevada casinos' take, with the nickel slots producing $1 billion annually. Today, slots take up 60 percent of casino floor space and generate more profits for the casinos than from all table games combined. Currently, casinos average about 3,000 slots apiece. The programming of the machines makes a jackpot rare enough for the big pay off, but still allows for a tidy profit for the casino. Most machines are set to pay out somewhere between 83 and 98 percent, but slot payoffs vary from one casino to another.

The phenomenal popularity of slot machines might be because they require no skill, and the pace can be set by the player. Players are driven by the idea that a machine will be ready to pay off after a certain amount of play, though in reality, payouts are completely random.

The Rio at twilight

The **Fremont Hotel and Casino** (www.fremontcasino. com) was one of Las Vegas' first high-rises, built in 1956, and is famous for launching Wayne Newton's career. The hotel no longer has a showroom, but 450 modest guest rooms were renovated in the latter part of last decade. The Fremont's block-long signage helps turn Downtown night into day, and the Second Street Grill is a hidden gem, featuring Pacific Rim specialties.

EL CORTEZ

Unrivaled for its continuous parade of low-stakes gamblers, **El Cortez Hotel and Casino** (built in 1941; http://el cortezhotelcasino.com) is the city's oldest continuously operating casino, but many of the rooms – especially the suites – have been renovated to keep up with the times. The relatively large casino still features single-deck blackjack, loose slots, and absurdly low limits, though many of the penny and nickel machines have been removed to make

Hard Rock Hotel and Casino

the floor less congested. Dining options include the classic steakhouse Siegel 1941. There are 364 rooms at remarkably low prices.

WEST OF THE STRIP

Las Vegas has been described as 'Des Moines with casinos,' and to a certain extent that is true – beyond the glitter of the Strip, the quality of attractions pales. But there are still intriguing stops worth a visitor's time and effort. While most hotel-casinos and resorts are concentrated along the Strip and within the Downtown area, some are found just off the Strip. To the west are more recently developed resort corridors off both Flamingo Road and Tropicana Avenue.

WEST FLAMINGO ROAD

Three noteworthy casinos are located on West Flamingo Road. The **Rio All-Suite Resort and Casino** ⑱ (www.caesars.com/rio-las-vegas) offers a variety of quality mid-priced amenities. There are 2,522 rooms in total, and the standard accommodations are among the largest in Vegas. The **Masquerade Village** is a Carnival-themed collection of gaming, retail outlets, and restaurants, while the **Voodoo Lounge** is a top-floor cocktail lounge with citywide views. The casino floor, lorded over by serious-looking pit bosses wearing laughably gaudy tropical wear, is packed with locals and tourists, especially on weekends. Five-dollar minimum bets are standard. This casino also hosts the World Series of Poker Main Event every year.

Worth a trip away from the Strip, the **Palms Casino Resort** ⓲ (www.palms.com) has an understated Polynesian theme and is decorated in soft beiges and taupes. Check out **Ghostbar** for stylish elegance, as well as the sensuous hotel pool and the tropical spa treatments. The hotel attracts well-heeled visitors, as well as a surprising number of locals. The Palms also boasts a full recording studio and a high-tech concert hall.

Offering a combination of entertainment and gaming, the **Gold Coast Hotel and Casino** (www.goldcoastcasino.com) fulfills many traditional Las Vegas expectations. On site is a 70-lane bowling center, a lounge with karaoke, and a dance

CONVENTIONS

The Las Vegas Convention Center is one of the largest convention centers in the world. The Consumer Electronics Show held in winter is a particularly popular event. Other major conventions include gatherings of the adult-entertainment industry, automobile accessory marketers, fashion companies, and even pizza-equipment industries.

The obvious financial benefit of the influx of conventioneers is offset by snarled traffic, inflated room rates, and packed attractions. Some merchants – and most taxi drivers – complain that conventioneers are less free-spending than vacationers. Nevertheless, city planners continue to woo the convention trade, with several Strip resorts building their own centers, and new ones springing up in the valley.

hall that regularly features live big-band, swing, and rocka-billy music. Dining rooms are varied and inexpensive, and the swimming pool is popular. But the true resort draw is in the huge number of video poker machines.

ORLEANS

The showy facade of the **Orleans Hotel and Casino** (www.orleanscasino.com) on West Tropicana Avenue is a little misleading and overbearing; once you enter, the decor is rather subtle. The casino is more akin to a warehouse than the Big Easy, but the 50-ft (15-m) ceilings do well to eradicate the typical smoky, claustrophobic atmosphere. A 70-lane bowling center and multi-screen movie theater attract locals, while the 15 restaurants, 9,000-seat arena, and the 850-seat show-room (featuring well-known music legends and comedians) should appeal to anyone seeking fun on a budget.

Automobile at the Nevada State Museum

EAST OF THE STRIP

For all its reputation as a vacation hot-spot, Las Vegas also enjoys success as a major convention destination. Every week companies, industries, and lifestyle organizations arrive en masse from all over the world to mix business with pleasure. How vital are such trade shows to the city economy? Enough so that many Las Vegas resorts

Old Mormon Fort Historic Park

– such as Mandalay Bay – have elaborate convention facilities, as do suburbs like Henderson.

The king of conventions, however, remains the **Las Vegas Convention Center** (www.lvcva.com). The facility boasts 3.2 million sq ft (297,000 sq m), 144 meeting rooms, and state-of-the-art technology. It is also within walking distance of more than 100,000 hotel rooms, one of the center's main attractions.

THE HARD ROCK

One of the more notable hotels in Las Vegas not located on the Strip is the **Hard Rock Hotel and Casino** ⑳ (www.hardrockhotel.com) on Paradise Road. If you're wondering where the hip and pretty people hang out, this is the place. Guitars of the stars and other music memorabilia are on display everywhere: there are vintage gold records on the walls, and some slot machine handles are shaped like Fender Stratocaster guitar necks. The music motif comes to life almost nightly in the 4,000-seat showroom, dubbed the Joint. Dining options range from casual to elegant, the

Vanity nightclub thumps until 4am on weekends, and a lush pool area recreates a tropical beach to greet sunbathers all summer long – especially at the drunken Rehab parties on Sundays. Rooms are modern and tasteful, with flat-screen TVs, and Bose sound systems.

CULTURAL ATTRACTIONS

Las Vegas is gunning hard to establish itself as a center for the arts, but even though the city's history is short, its past is not being neglected. There are several institutes devoted to Las Vegas history, but the best of the bunch is the **Las Vegas Springs Preserve ㉑** (333 South Valley View Boulevard; tel: 702-822 7700; www.springspreserve.org; daily 10am–6pm). This multi-faceted facility is home to the **Origen Museum**, an interactive look at the area's past; the **Desert Living Center**, a five-building complex that focuses on sustainable living in the desert; and a host of gardens and trails; and the **Nevada State Museum and Historical Society**.

Neon Museum

The **Las Vegas Natural History Museum** (900 Las Vegas Boulevard North; tel: 702-384 3466; www.lvnhm.org; daily 9am–4pm) is large on reptiles and snakes. Visitors to the **Old Mormon Fort Historic**

Park (500 East Washington Avenue; tel: 702-486 3511; Mon–Fri 8am–5pm) can see remnants of the city's oldest building, a fort built by original Mormon settlers in 1855. There's plenty to engage adults, too, at the **Lied Discovery Children's Museum** (833 Las Vegas Boulevard North; tel: 702-382 3445; www.discovery kidslv.org; June–Aug Mon–Sat 10am–5pm, Sun noon–5pm; Sept–May Tue–Fri 9am–4pm, Sat 10am–5pm, Sun noon–5pm).

University of Nevada at Las Vegas

Also not to be missed, the **Neon Museum** ㉒ (tel: 702-387 6366; www.neonmuseum.org; day and night tours), which has rescued and refurbished hundreds of historic neon signs since 1996. The collection here consists of three components: the Fremont Street Gallery, the Neon Signs Project, and the Boneyard. All of these are located Downtown. The first two parts of the collection are working signs (and therefore available for viewing 24 hours a day). Tours of the Boneyard, home to 100 additional signs, are available by appointment only.

ART MUSEUMS

At the Bellagio is one of the classiest museums in the West, the **Bellagio Gallery of Fine Art** (tel: 702-693 7871; daily 10am–8pm). The hall presents intimate temporary exhibitions featuring work from some of the world's most compelling artists.

THE UNIVERSITY OF NEVADA, LAS VEGAS

The **University of Nevada at Las Vegas** (UNLV) and the **Community College of Southern Nevada** have been unofficial outposts of beyond-the-neon culture since their inception. UNLV's sprawling urban campus on South Maryland Parkway has quite a collection of interesting sights and venues.

The **Marjorie Barrick Museum** (tel: 702-895 3381; Mon–Fri, 9am–5pm, Sat noon–5pm, Sept–Apr Thu until 8pm) has some good exhibits on the arts and crafts of the Paiute, Navajo, and Mexican Native Americans. It also houses the collection of the Las Vegas Art Museum. Just outside the entrance is the campus **Xeric Garden**, a landscaped sampling of desert plants in a beautiful setting.

The **Donna Beam Fine Arts Gallery** (tel: 702-895 3893, Mon–Fri 9am–5pm) is a spacious hall exhibiting the work of students as well as professionals. Also on campus is the **Artemus Ham Concert Hall**, featuring classical, rock, and theatrical performances, and the **Thomas and Mack Center** (www.thomasand mack.com), an arena with 18,000 seats, that hosts everything from hockey to rodeos and musical events. On the Community College campus at 3200 East Cheyenne Avenue is the city's only

Lake Mead and the Hoover Dam

planetarium (tel: 702-651 4759), where the latest digital technology is used to project views of planets and stars, as well as 3D films, onto the domed screen.

EXCURSIONS

HOOVER DAM AND LAKE MEAD

There is much to do within easy driving distance of Las Vegas, from recreation to sightseeing. The top draw is the **Hoover Dam** ㉓, responsible for Las Vegas's first major crowd (of 20,000), who attended its 1935 dedication. Long

after its completion, the dam remains an awe-inspiring sight.

Striking sculptures by Oskar J.W. Hansen may be the largest monumental bronzes ever cast in the US. A dizzying 725ft (526m) high, this engineering marvel straddles the Nevada-Arizona border a half-hour's drive south of Las Vegas on US93. The **Hoover Dam Visitors Center** (tel: 702-494-2517; www.usbr.gov/lc/hooverdam; daily 9am–5pm) has exhibits on the history of the dam's construction and a viewing platform. The one million visitors who come here each year can choose between the 30-minute Powerplant Tour (9.25am–3.55pm) and the 1-hour Hoover Dam Tour (9.30am–3.30pm), which includes guided access to the passageways within the dam itself. Visitors can expect the same kind of security screening they'd get at an international airport. No pets are allowed.

Serene Lake Mead

The result of building the Hoover Dam, **Lake Mead National Recreation Area** ㉔ offers more than 500 miles (800km) of shoreline in the midst of a 1.5-million-acre (607,000-hectare) national recreation area. A popular spot for locals and visitors alike, America's largest man-made body of water is open all year (peak usage month is June). Activities include fishing, swimming, water-skiing, boating, self-guided hiking, camping, and picnicking. Boats can be rented at the **Lake Mead Marina** (www.boatinglakemead. com). **Lake Mead Cruises** (tel: 702-293 6180; www.2lake meadcruises.com; ask about hotel pick-up) offers a variety of excursions, including a sunset dinner cruise aboard a vintage paddlewheeler. The company can schedule trips around the lake on Jet Skis, as well as on a fast-paced jet-boat that heads in the direction of the Grand Canyon. The lake is best reached through Henderson, 10–15 minutes from the Strip by freeway, or Boulder City, a half-hour drive south of Las Vegas.

BOULDER CITY

Boulder City itself is an anomaly in Nevada – a city that rejects gaming and discourages excessive growth. Its small-town feel is quaint and charming by the standards of booming suburban southern Nevada.

The heart of the town is a historic square, fronted by 1930s-era buildings such as the **Boulder Dam Hotel** (www.boulderdamhotel.com) and the **Boulder Theatre** (www.bouldertheater.com). The town is also home to several art galleries and antiques shops. Also worth seeing is the **Boulder City Hoover Dam Museum** (tel: 702-294 1988; www.bcmha.org; Mon–Sat 10am–5pm), which is well-stocked with artifacts from the building of the dam and the founding of Boulder City. In the fall, several festivals, including Art in the Park and Damboree (a celebration of the town's heritage), entice thousands to abandon the gaming tables and make the trek from Las Vegas. Take US93 south about 25 miles (40km) from Vegas; Hoover Dam is an additional 7 miles (11km).

GHOST TOWNS

While not really a ghost town, **Goodsprings** has the feel of a genuinely spooky place. The functioning homes are surrounded by mill foundations and abandoned mine operations. The hamlet's chief attraction is the Pioneer Saloon,

the country's largest stamped-metal building. Head south from Las Vegas on Interstate 15 and turn at the tiny town of **Jean**.

The true and authentic ghost town of **Rhyolite** is located 126 miles (200km) northwest of Las Vegas on US95. This town was once Nevada's second-largest city, thanks to a 1904 gold strike. Remnants of this grandeur can be seen in the Tonopah Las Vegas Railroad depot. A top attraction is the bottle house, built of 50,000 glass bottles, a common practice in the days when building supplies were scarce.

VALLEY OF FIRE STATE PARK

Fifty miles (80km) northeast of Las Vegas via Interstate 15 (watch for the Valley of Fire exit, State Route 169), **Valley of Fire State Park ㉕** is a spectacular alien landscape of erosion-sculpted, brilliant red sandstone. The park features petroglyphs dating to 300 BC, most accessible by light hikes. Atlatl Rock has a stairway to the carvings, while the glyphs at Mouse's Tank require an easy 0.25-mile (0.5-km) trek. For the car-bound, there is a 6-mile (9.5-km) scenic loop through White Domes, a stunning vista of sandstone formations that were once the bottom of an inland sea. There are also some picnic areas

Tract housing by Lake Mead in Boulder

and overnight campgrounds. The park is best visited in late spring or fall.

In nearby Overton, the **Lost City Museum** (721 South Moapa Valley Boulevard; tel: 702-397 2193; daily 8.30am–4.30pm) preserves the ruins of Pueblo Grande de Nevada, the state's largest ancient Anasazi community, which was moved here brick by adobe brick before its original site was flooded by Lake Mead.

RED ROCK CANYON

Red Rock Canyon National Conservation Area ㉖, a half-hour drive west of downtown Las Vegas via Charleston Boulevard, is a dramatic vista of mountains and colorful sheer rock faces. Rather than just a single canyon, it is a 13-mile (21-km) ridge with canyons eroded into its flanks. First stop should be the **Red Rock Visitors Center** (tel: 702-515 5350;

Desert shack in Rhyolite, a ghost town

daily 8am–4.30pm), which has archaeological displays and dioramas depicting the lives of early native inhabitants. At Willow Spring, well-preserved petroglyphs can still be seen.

Skywalk over the Grand Canyon

Starting at the center, a one-way scenic loop meanders through the area's stunning topography. When driving on the loop, watch out for bicyclists. Picnicking spaces are plentiful, as are hiking trails of varying levels of difficulty. During migratory seasons, bird watchers can have a field day. The canyon is one of the nation's top rock-climbing sites, with an almost endless variety of ascents, but novices should stick to an appropriate level; rescuers are frequently called out to help lost or injured visitors.

MOUNT CHARLESTON

For a cool break from the desert, try 11,918-ft (3,631-m) **Charleston Peak**, near the town of **Mount Charleston**, 40 minutes north of Las Vegas on US95. Two areas command particular attention: Kyle Canyon and Lee Canyon. Kyle is home to scenic Cathedral Rock, Mary Jane Falls, and Big Falls, all accessible by trail (Cathedral Rock requires a three-hour trek). Lee Canyon is home to a ski and snowboarding resort, remarkable for being so near the desert. The mountain features numerous scenic overlooks and picnicking sites, while the ranger station on Kyle Canyon Road can provide advice.

Bryce Canyon, with Thor's Hammer

GRAND CANYON

There are several noteworthy national parks within driving distance of Las Vegas. The most famous and most popular is **Grand Canyon National Park** ㉗. The North Rim is 280 miles (448km) east of Las Vegas; the South Rim 260 miles (416km) from Vegas. There are no connecting bridges across the divide. The **South Rim**, accessible by Interstate 40 through the state of Arizona, is the most visited area of the park. It is also closest to the **Skywalk**, an awe-inspiring glass-floored platform suspended 4,000 ft (1,200 m) above the Colorado River. The **North Rim** – arrived at by Interstate 15 through St George, Utah – receives a fraction of that traffic because of the longer journey times. The stunning natural wonder makes an ideal excursion far away from Sin City's glitz. Driving there is the preferable option, because having a car gives you access to outstanding scenic overlooks and access to good walking trails, although they are narrow and close to the edge, so agility is desirable. For anyone in a hurry, it's possible to take an organized airplane or helicopter charter trip and return to Vegas the same day.

For active travelers, the park offers backpacking, rafting, and mule-back descents into the canyon. Back-country hiking requires an advance permit; hikes down to the river generally take two days or more, and returning even longer. For more sedentary visitors, there are historic sites to visit, star-gazing, bird-watching, and, of course, enough spectacular scenery to keep all eyes constantly busy. To travel down into the canyon, make all your arrangements well in advance.

As for weather, both rims receive snow in the winter, and even summer evenings may be chilly. Due to climate conditions, the North Rim is usually open from May to October. Down in the canyon, more desert-like conditions prevail, with summer afternoons approaching 120°F (49°C). For more information, tel: 928-638 7888, www.nps.gov/grca, or contact

GRAND CANYON

One of the world's most spectacular natural phenomena, the Grand Canyon averages 10 miles (16km) wide and reaches depths of 5,700ft (1,700m). It transects five of the seven temperate zones, each with its own unique ecology. Declared a National Park in 1919, the canyon was first seen by Lieutenant Joseph Ives in 1857, who called it a 'pointless locality.'

The canyon has been created over millions of years by the erosion of the great Colorado River. From the lookout points at the rim of the canyon, the river seems little more than a trickling stream. Climbing within designated areas is encouraged: strata of red-and-yellow sandstone sandwich layers of dark granite and pale limestone, revealing the surrounding Earth's structure and layers of evolution.

the Las Vegas Convention and Visitors Authority, tel: 702-892 0711, www.lvcva.com.

ZION AND BRYCE CANYON NATIONAL PARKS

Northeast, in Utah, are the spectacular Zion and Bryce Canyon national parks. Around 155 miles (248km) from Las Vegas, en route to the North Rim of the Grand Canyon, **Zion Canyon** offers natural wonders such as stark rock formations, sheer cliff faces, slot canyons, and rippling waterfalls. The park, accessible year-round, offers hiking trails and scenic drives.

Farther north – 210 miles (336km) from Las Vegas – is **Bryce Canyon**, an amazing series of natural amphitheaters scooped from the edge of the Paunsagunt Plateau by the Paria River. Bryce is known for its colorful formations of sculptured rock – pinnacles, pedestals, fins, and spires. Sinking Ship, Thor's Hammer, and Natural Bridge (an awesome arch of rock) are just a sample of the canyon's spectacular geological sights.

DEATH VALLEY
Death Valley National Park ㉘, presumed to be the last resting place of many a gold and silver prospector, is 145 miles (232km) west of Las Vegas. Take US95 northwest or Interstate 15 south to Baker, California to get there. Death Valley's many popular destinations include Furnace Creek (which, with a gas station, hotels, and a golf course, is the only dot of civilization), the Devil's Golf Course, Zabriskie Point (immortalized in an art-house movie of the same name), and the improbable Spanish-Mediterranean Scotty's Castle, completed in 1931 and which required the labor of 2,000 workers. The **Death Valley National Park Visitors Center** (tel: 760-786 3200) can provide maps and information.

Sand dunes in Death Valley

WHAT TO DO

From circuses to cocktail bars, roller coasters to rock 'n' roll, the list is endless. Gambling may be the main event, but the sideshows can be spectacular.

Cirque du Soleil set a trend by having an auditorium built specifically for its fabulous show. Las Vegas resident Celine Dion soon followed; the Colosseum theater opened at Caesars Palace designed exclusively for her act. While the big shows mean big money for the resorts, this hasn't always been the case. When Elvis started his 1969 residency at the International (which later became the Las Vegas Hilton), it was reportedly the first time that a casino made a profit in the showroom.

Las Vegas reaps the rewards and suffers the losses of a metropolis of over two million residents whose primary industry is tourism. This makes the traditional travelers' definitions of 'what to do' and 'where to go' difficult to delineate. In this town, the two overlap. Casinos, resorts, gambling, and entertainment: Where does one stop and the next begin? In Sin City they are interrelated, interconnected, and interdependent.

With the overwhelming population explosion that started in the late 1980s came a demand from the locals for more traditional, off-Strip experiences, sparking a growth in culture, sports, and amenities. Locals and visitors are each feeling their way along a new path for experiencing Las Vegas, one that combines the expected attractions of the gaming and tourism industry with those types of independent cultural and sports amenities found in a more traditional city. The result is a surprising combination.

GAMBLING

Since 1931, when gambling was officially legalized in Nevada after 22 years of prohibition, it has been used to promote the

Rollercoaster ride at New York New York resort and casino

Collect your chips

Many casinos issue special chips for events like New Year, and players often prefer to collect them rather than cash them in.

city. Without question, the primary allure of Las Vegas – despite the resorts, restaurants, showrooms, and shopping malls – is the fact that you can legally place bets on games of chance and sporting events. Make no mistake: the times may be changing, but without gambling, there would be no Forum Shops, no replicas of world-famous landmarks, and no dancing fountains.

Most of the gambling in Las Vegas is concentrated along the Strip, where nearly 25 major casinos in excess of 100,000 sq ft (9,300 sq m) beckon passers-by to lighten their pockets and take the chance that they may be among the few who will win big.

At most gaming tables along the Strip, action is fast and furious, with generally inflexible house rules. Downtown casinos are a bit more flexible when it comes to house rules, offering lower minimums and higher limits. This attracts the unlikely combination of serious career gamblers and novices without much to spend. Still, the atmosphere is generally more relaxed and amiable, probably due to the fact that Downtown is a concentrated area similar to a small town – one that has not changed much in 80 years. Still, before you venture into any live gaming area, it is important to familiarize yourself with the rules of the game.

Despite the exceptions mentioned above, most experienced gamblers have little patience for the novice, as they see them as a bad omen in the already frustrating situation of having to beat odds that are against them. Also, there are strict rules regarding what the player should do with their cards and chips, and where they can place their hands. Disobeying these rules can cost you a bet on the low end; repeated violations can lead to expulsion from the casino.

CARD SCHOOLS

If you are completely inexperienced, there are several ways to overcome your lack of knowledge. The first is to read about the games. (Below is a very brief guide to the most popular games.) Another method is to practice on the video versions of these games before moving to live table action. With no other players waiting impatiently for you to make your next move, electronic gaming is an alternative that many novice gamblers never move beyond. Most casinos offer a variety of video game machines.

Despite the potentially intimidating aspects of live gaming, it makes little sense to spend your vacation in Las Vegas and not play at least a few hands of blackjack or craps, especially when there are free gaming lessons offered at several different casinos. This hands-on method is the best way to learn a game and its rules without risking your money or pride.

Casino chips

BACCARAT

Typically assumed to be a high-roller card game, baccarat *(bah-cah-rah)* is similar to blackjack, though it's played with stricter rules, higher limits, and less player interaction. The object of the game is to come as close as possible to 9; the only real skill involved is deciding whether to bet on the player or the bank (ie the dealer).

Most baccarat tables are located in quiet, sequestered sections of the casino. Gambling lessons are highly recommended for this game.

BINGO

Nearly everyone knows the game of bingo, the mini-lottery in which players try to line up a horizontal or a vertical row of randomly drawn numbers. The numbers are called out until someone wins; a few veterans get up to 10 cards playing at once. No lessons required.

BLACKJACK (OR 21)

This is the most popular live table game in Las Vegas – and the easiest card game to learn – due to its relative simplicity. The object is to play against the dealer (house) and draw cards as close to 21 as possible without busting (going over 21). There are several optional bets – splitting, doubling down, insurance (never take insurance) – and variations that include single-deck vs. multi-deck card shoes, and hands dealt face-up (as opposed to one card down). The house advantage is that if you bust, the dealer takes your money even if he busts too.

Margaritaville owner Jimmy Buffett at The Flamingo

BLACKJACK SWITCH

Introduced to the Vegas scene in 2010, this blackjack-derivative game requires betters to play two hands at a time, and allows them to switch top cards between hands. If you think all that switching gives players an extra advantage, you're right. That's precisely

A craps casino table

why blackjacks only pay even money, and why all bets push when the dealer gets 22.

CRAPS

This is the raucous game of cheering (and cursing) crowds, where everyone at the table has a stake in what one hapless gambler does with the dice. Loud players, dramatically placed chips, and flying dice all revolve around a set of complex betting rules, and the fact that 7 is more likely to be rolled than any other number. Bets are placed for and against the dice thrower (or shooter). Money changes hands very quickly at a craps table, making it another candidate for lessons, but it's not as complicated as it looks. Don't lean against a craps table unless you know what you're doing, or have plenty of money to lose.

PAI GOW

If you enjoy poker, gambling at a mild pace, and playing against a slim house advantage, you'll love Pai Gow. Each player is dealt seven cards, which are then arranged by the player into two piles: one five-card hand and one two-card hand. Standard poker rules apply; that is, pairs, straights, flushes, and full houses are ranked in a hierarchy of hands to determine the winner. The five-card hand must beat the two-card hand, and both hands must beat the dealer's two hands in order to win. If only one of the dealer's hands wins, the game is a push (tie), and no money changes hands (this happens more often than not). If both the dealer's hands win, you lose. It's perfectly acceptable to ask the dealer for advice on how to play your hand (and a great way to learn). The caveat is that since the house has only a slim advantage, it takes 5 percent of your winnings.

POKER

A high-stakes card game played in a high-pressure atmosphere. Unlike most other card games, gamblers here play against each other; the house operates the game for a fixed percentage of each pot, usually 5 percent. There are many variations on offer, from the standard 7-card stud to Texas Hold 'Em. If you're new to the game, this might be an expensive place to learn. If you can't figure out who the fish (poor players) at the table are, you might be one of them.

Luck of the dice

ROULETTE

A subdued game of European flair, roulette is a relatively simple game, where bets are placed by laying chips on a single number or groups of numbers, colors, or even/odd. Different players are given different colored chips to avoid confusion. The wheel is spun, the ball drops, and where it lands determines the outcome. Odds are as high as 35 to 1, which means a single $5 chip on the right number wins $175. Avoid playing a double-zero wheel and search for those with only one zero.

SLOT MACHINES

Slot machines at Planet Hollywood

Slot machines have become the most popular form of gaming in Las Vegas – so much so that they supersede the play at table games in many casinos. Though all modern slot machines are computerized, the rules are the same: get three or four matching icons in a row (or some combination thereof) and you win. The difference is that the computer decides when you win, not pure chance. And even though the payback increases with the more you bet on a single pull, the computer will decrease your odds of winning. The skill, they say, is to find a slot machine that's hitting, that is, a computer that's programmed to pay out big money.

THREE-CARD POKER

This poker-derivative game is one of the most popular casino diversions of all time. Players ante-in for three cards, which are distributed randomly by a computerized shuffler. From these cards, they must make a poker hand that beats the dealer. To

A hand of poker

tangle with the dealer, players must match their original bets. The dealer only pays winners if he or she qualifies; that is, has a queen or better. Players also may wager at the outset on whether their cards will comprise a bonus hand. These hands, essentially straights or better, pay odds of 2 to 1 and higher.

VIDEO POKER

Video poker has become increasingly popular, so much so that there's hardly a bar, grocery store, or laundromat in Las Vegas that doesn't have at least two or three machines. It's the same as regular five-card draw, with the machine acting as dealer. Unlike slots, interaction and a semblance of skill are required; you are offered a choice on how to play the hand you're dealt. A chart on the screen lists the payoff of your winning hand and, as with slots, the more you bet, the better the payoff. Versions of video poker range from Jacks or Better (the standard game) to Double Bonus or Deuces Wild, although the more wild cards involved, the lower the payoff. Some casinos now also offer video blackjack and roulette.

THE BIG SHOWS

Once, Las Vegas showrooms were filled with top-notch entertainment – headliners, comedians, production shows, and dancing girls – all at a very low price. In that bygone era, elaborate dinner shows were seen by the casinos as a loss leader, a way to keep customers happily dropping money at the tables or the slot machines. As long as the bottom line was glittering, the casino operators, especially during the days of the mob, were happy to continue providing entertainment and food very inexpensively, or even for free.

When corporations moved in with more stringent departmental accounting procedures, every sector of a hotel-casino had to show success. Not satisfied with a simple overall profit, corporate operators began to raise prices and cut corners, resulting in an era of frustrating mediocrity from which Las Vegas has only recently emerged.

Now, most showrooms are again offering quality stars and elaborate productions, without the accompanying dinner service. Prices have certainly risen, but so has the benchmark of quality. Some of the bigger shows and headliner appearances (especially during major events like New Year's Eve) cost more than $100 per ticket – typical for New York, but previously unheard of in Las Vegas. What this means is that, in the case of showroom entertainers, the old adage of 'getting what you pay for' now applies to Las Vegas.

Celine Dion at the Colosseum

KEEPING UP WITH THE SHOWS
Although the runs for the shows listed here – with the exception of most headliner performances – are considered open-ended, remember

that nothing is static in Las Vegas. Entire resorts open and close, and showrooms frequently change show times, prices, or featured productions. Also, there are numerous headlining entertainers who change from week to week. For current listings of all the entertainment around town, pick up a copy of *Las Vegas Magazine* (http://lasvegasmagazine.com) or *What's On: The Las Vegas Guide* (http://whats-on.com), the two most comprehensive listings guides. In the reviews below, 'dark' refers to the day when the show does not play at all. Please remember that it is tradition for showgirls in Las Vegas shows to be topless, so some of the shows are not appropriate for children.

Blue Man Group: This award-winning show features three bald, blue characters who play drums, splash paint, and toilet-paper the audience. The one-of-a-kind showroom experience has been called innovative, hilarious, and musically powerful. Luxor Hotel and Casino, 3900 Las Vegas Boulevard South, tel: 702-262 4444, www.luxor.com. Shows daily 4pm, 7pm, or 9.30pm.

Blue Man Group poster at the Venetian

Jennifer Lopez: A new headliner in Las Vegas, J.Lo performs all the hits with her trademark Latin flair in the intimate, nightclub-like Axis Theater. The Axis at Planet Hollywood, 3667 Las Vegas Boulevard South, tel: 702-777-2782, www.caesars.

com/planet-hollywood. Shows 9pm; days vary.

Cirque du Soleil KÀ: This martial arts-heavy iteration of Cirque du Soleil's magic tells the story of twins on their journey to fulfil a shared destiny. MGM Grand Hotel and Casino, 3799 Las Vegas Boulevard South; tel: 702-531 3826, www.mgm grand.com. Shows 7pm and 9.30pm; dark Thu–Fri.

Cirque du Soleil Zarkana

Cirque du Soleil Love: Originally conceived by the late George Harrison and his friend, Cirque founder Guy Laliberté, this celebration of the Beatles' songs features psychedelic lighting, rare and remastered music and, of course, amazing acrobatics. The Mirage, 3400 Las Vegas Boulevard South, tel: 702-792-7777, www.mirage.com. Shows 7pm and 9.30pm; dark Tue–Wed.

Cirque du Soleil Michael Jackson: One: This spectacular show is a tribute to the king of pop, featuring such enduring hits as *Bad, Beat It* and *Smooth Criminal*. A must for all Michael Jackson fans. Mandalay Bay Resort and Casino, 3950 Las Vegas Boulevard South, tel: 877-632-7400, www.mandalay-bay.com. Shows 7pm and 9.30pm; dark Wed–Thu.

Cirque du Soleil Mystère: This popular show was the Cirque's first in Las Vegas, and the modern spin on a traditional circus remains a unique experience that borders on performance art. TI (Treasure Island), 3300 Las Vegas Boulevard South, tel: 702-894 7722. Shows 7pm and 9.30pm; dark Mon–Tue.

Cirque du Soleil O: From the acclaimed international troupe, *O* dazzles audiences in an aquatic environment that utilizes about 1.5 million gallons (6.8 million liters) of water. Around

Britney Spears at the Linq Promenade

75 highly skilled acrobats – all scuba-certified – dive, swim, and perform trapeze and high-wire acts in a remarkable auditorium. Bellagio, 3600 Las Vegas Boulevard South, tel: 702-693 8866. Shows 7.30pm and 10pm; dark Mon–Tue.

Cirque du Soleil Zarkana: This acrobatic fantasy spins a story of a magician who lost both his power and love. Aria Resort and Casino, 3730 Las Vegas Boulevard South; tel: 855-927 5262, www.aria.com. Shows 7pm and 9.30pm; dark Sun–Mon.

Cirque du Soleil Zumanity: The fine Canadian corps presents an adult-themed, erotic evening showcasing human sensuality, arousal, and eroticism with 50 performers, including acrobats, contortionists and magicians. New York-New York Las Vegas Hotel and Casino, 3790 Las Vegas Boulevard South, tel: 866-815 4365, www.newyorknewyork.com. Shows 7pm and 9.30pm; dark Sun–Mon.

Celine Dion: After three years of sell-outs in the Colosseum at Caesars Palace and a brief hiatus in 2014, Celine has returned to sing all the favorites. Caesars Palace, 3570 Las

Vegas Boulevard South, tel: 866-574 3851, www.thecolos-
seum.com. Shows 7.30pm; dark Mon.

Terry Fator: Ventriloquism hits the big-time in this rollicking
show that features reality-show winner Mr Fator. While most of
the act is funny, the puppeteer is at his best when he impersons-
ates music legends such as Guns N' Roses, Garth Brooks and
Gnarls Barkley. The Mirage, 3400 Las Vegas Boulevard South,
tel: 702-792 7777, www.mirage.com. Shows 7.30pm; Mon–Thu.

Jersey Boys: The music of Frankie Valli and the Four Seasons
comprises the soundtrack for this show, which is popular
among those who were alive in the 1950s, when the musical
group rose to stardom. The Paris Las Vegas, 3655 Las Vegas
Boulevard South, tel: 702-777 2782, www.caesars.com/paris-
las-vegas. Show times vary; dark Mon.

Jubilee!: Long before the blockbuster movie, Donn Arden's
Jubilee! was sinking the *Titanic* on the Strip in what is the
show's amazing signature special effect. The production also
features dozens of topless and costumed showgirls, making
this an event – in true Las Vegas tradition – for adults only.
Bally's Las Vegas, 3645 Las Vegas Boulevard South; tel: 702-
777 2782, www.caesars.com/ballys-las-vegas. Shows 7pm
and 9.30pm; dark Fri.

The Million Dollar Piano: In 2015, Elton John celebrated the
100th performance of this dazzling sentimental show in which
the namesake piano dominates the stage and he sings all his
favorites. Caesars Palace, 3570 Las Vegas Boulevard South,
tel: 888-929 7849, www.thecolosseum.com. Shows 7.30pm;
dark Thu and Sun.

Penn & Teller: The dynamic magic duo entertains in an epony-
mous theater in the Rio Hotel, performing new tricks, exposing
how old ones are done, and generally being genial. Rio All-
Suite Hotel and Casino, 3700 West Flamingo Road; tel: 702-777
2782, www.caesars.com/rio-las-vegas. Shows 9pm; dark Fri.

Le Rêve: Subtitled 'a Small Collection of Imperfect Dreams,' this is a visually stunning journey into the world of sleep, set in and around a huge tank of water which serves as a stage. Note: visitors in the first three rows of the audience might get wet. Wynn Las Vegas, 3131 Las Vegas Boulevard South; tel: 702-770 9966, www.wynnlasvegas.com. Shows 7pm and 9.30pm; dark Wed–Thu.

Tournament of Kings: A classic dinner show and great fun for families: a recreation of a medieval knights' jousting tournament, with swooning maidens and fearsome dragons galore. Excalibur Hotel and Casino, 3850 Las Vegas Boulevard South; tel: 702-597 76000, www.excalibur.com. Shows 6pm and/or 8.30pm; dark Tue.

ADULT ENTERTAINMENT

For all the hype about Las Vegas's conversion to a family town, the truth is that beyond all the shiny big-name properties lies a bevy of adult-oriented distractions. In recent years efforts have been made to eliminate the seediest and most disreputable of these, while those operating within the law have flourished. As a result, Las Vegas seems ready to accept the multiple layers of complexity its status as a tourist city throws up.

Many of the resorts on the Strip have appeased family visitors by cleaning up their shows and covering up their show-girls. The long-running *Jubilee!* show at **Bally's** still has some of the girls topless.

The most popular shows on the Strip today are girls'-night-out male stripper shows such as *Chippendales* at the **Rio** (www.chippendales.com) and *Thunder from Down Under* at the **Excalibur** (www.thunderfromdownunder.com).

There are dozens of clubs other than casinos that offer either nude or topless entertainment. Most of the topless-only clubs have full bars. For totally nude dancers, the choices are just as varied, but due to Vegas' complicated licensing laws, most do not serve alcohol. For both drinks and skin (male or female), try the **Spearmint Rhino**, 3340 Highland Drive, spearmintrhinolv.com, or **Cheetah's**, 2112 Western Avenue, www.cheetahslasvegas.com. **Girls of Glitter Gulch**, 20 Fremont Street, is as historic as it is titillating, and is the sexiest attraction in the Fremont Street Experience.

NIGHTLIFE

From local bars featuring live music and comedy to nightclubs and music venues, the city's after-dusk life beyond gambling and shows is very healthy.

For a detailed listing of local events beyond the Strip, pick up one of the two free alternative newsweeklies, *Vegas Seven* (http://vegasseven.com) or *Las Vegas Weekly* (http://las vegasweekly.com).

The Vesper Bar at the Cosmopolitan of Las Vegas

NIGHTCLUBS AND BARS

After the heady days of the 1950s, nightclubbing took a nose-dive but is popular again, thanks to a resurgence of dance music. This has led to a deluge of hotel-based high-energy clubs, including **Marquee** (http://marqueelasvegas.com) in the Cosmopolitan, **Vanity** in the Hard Rock and **Tao** in the Venetian. The Venetian's

DJ Chris Gilmore of Incubus performing at The Joint

sister property, the Palazzo, is home to **Lavo** (http://lavolv.com), which is part restaurant, part club. Each hotspot caters to a specific crowd, so hunt around until you find the one for you.

Swanky bars – also known as Ultra-Lounges – have become a trend in recent years, and just about every casino resort has added one. Some of the best: **The Chandelier** and **Vesper Bar** inside the Cosmopolitan, **Revolution** at the Mirage, and **Savile Row** inside the Luxor. **Mandarin Bar**, an exquisite lounge on the 23rd floor of the Mandarin Oriental Las Vegas, also is worth a visit – if not for the view, then for the Champagne.

GAY CLUBS
Gays and lesbians can find much integrated nightlife in the so-called Fruit Loop area on Paradise Road. Popular venues include **Krave** (www.sharenightclub.com), **Pirnaha** (http://piranhavegas.com), and **Share** (www.sharenightclub.com). For information on local LGBT events visit http://lasvegaspride.org.

MUSIC VENUES

Vegas has live music venues to fit all tastes and budgets. Two local spots, where you are as likely to spy a real resident as you are an intrepid tourist sneaking away from the Strip, are the **Sam Boyd Stadium** (www.samboydstadium.com), an outdoor venue for big-ticket acts, and the **Thomas and Mack Center** (www.thomasandmack.com) on the University of Nevada at Las Vegas campus, hosting music as well as sports events. The **Las Vegas Arena** (www.arenalasvegas.com), due to open in 2016, is set to become a major sports and entertainment venue.

Never to be outdone, the big resorts also cater to music fans. The largest venue is the MGM Grand **Garden Arena**, modeled after New York City's Madison Square Garden. Home of the Billboard Music Awards, shows from the Garden starring Britney or Elton are likely to turn up on cable TV.

The popular Mandalay Bay **Events Center** showcases everyone from rock shows to opera stars, but arrive early to avoid the long entry lines. Large seats and spacious rows make the 9,000-seater **Orleans Arena** (inside the Orleans Hotel and Casino; www.orleansarena.com) a very comfortable venue, or catch a Broadway show or recording artist at the **The Axis** (inside Planet Hollywood). Another great casino-based music venue that is as classy and hip as anywhere in the US: The Hard Rock Casino's 4,000-seat **The Joint**, with probably the best sound system in the city. For a more intimate vibe, try **Book & Stage** inside the sports book at the Cosmopolitan.

Elvis impersonator

SHOPPING

Where there is money, there is shopping, and shopping facilities have always been around in Vegas. Over the past decade, everything has been kicked up a notch, with more luxury and high-end boutiques opening on the Strip. You can still find a bargain, but you might have to hunt a little harder to get past all the name brands.

SHOPPING MALLS

The **Forum Shops**, located at Caesars Palace, was the first themed indoor shopping promenade, built to look and feel like an outdoor Roman street. It surprised quite a few observers in 1992 by attracting not only the obvious tourists from the

WEDDINGS

Getting married almost ranks as a sport in Las Vegas, America's favorite city in which to tie the knot. More than 100,000 couples take the plunge here every year. Dozens of celebrities, including Michael Jordan, Elvis Presley, Britney Spears, and Richard Gere, have exchanged vows in Vegas; many of the chapels on Las Vegas Boulevard and Main Street have signs boasting of the big names they've joined in matrimony.

Most weddings are anything but traditional. You can use the drive-up wedding window at **A Little White Wedding Chapel** (www.alittlewhitechapel.com), have an Elvis impersonator sing your nuptials at the **Graceland Wedding Chapel** (www.gracelandchapel.com), have a fantasy-themed, for example gothic or zombie, ceremony at the **Viva Las Vegas Weddings** (www.vivalasvegasweddings.com), or get married in a helicopter over the Strip. Other options range from a bungee-jumping ceremony to saying your vows on a boat on Lake Mead.

Strip, but also more than a handful of shopping-starved locals eager to explore stores they once had to travel out-of-state to visit. The number of restaurants and entertainment outlets made the Forum a great place for an all-day, one-stop spending spree, and fueled the trend for others.

An ornate ceiling at Grand Canal Shoppes

Rivaling the Forum Shops in size, **Miracle Mile** (www.miraclemileshopslv.com), adjacent to Planet Hollywood, specializes in second locations of unique non-chain retail stores from around the US in a sleek setting that retains vestiges of the former Desert Passage mall. Most recently, Crystals (www.theshopsatcrystals.com), at CityCenter, has ratcheted the shopping up another notch, with outposts of Tom Ford, Gucci, and the first North American flagship of TAG Heuer.

Other hotels have taken similar approaches. Upscale stores like Tiffany, Versace, and Prada dominate **Via Bellagio** at Bellagio, while the **Grand Canal Shoppes** is a major part of the Venetian's centerpiece attraction. **The Encore Esplanade** at Wynn contains suitably high-end stores, as well.

The Fashion Show Mall (www.thefashionshow.com) is the largest non-casino shopping destination on the Strip, attracting good key stores such as Saks, Louis Vuitton, Macy's, and Nordstrom. South of the casinos, near McCarran International Airport, **Town Square Las Vegas** (www.mytownsquarelasvegas.com) provides open-air shopping in a contrived, new-Urbanist landscape.

Crystals shopping center

FACTORY OUTLET MALLS

Not far away from the Strip (although you will need a car or taxi) is **Las Vegas Premium Outlets South** (www.premiumoutlets.com), an outdoor mall with some 140 stores offering bargain opportunities ranging from clothing to electronics. On the way to Downtown, its sister property **Las Vegas Premium Outlets North** is home to 435,000 sq ft (40,000 sq m) of shopping in an upscale, village setting, located just off Interstate 15 and Charleston Boulevard.

The **Fashion Outlets of Las Vegas** (www.fashionoutletlasvegas.com) at Primm, Nevada (on the California state line) is one of the best of the outlet malls. It's a 30-minute drive on Interstate 15 (there is a shuttle bus from the Venetian resort, Miracle Mile Shops at Planet Hollywood and the Tropicana; tel: 1-888-424 6898), but the selection of top names (including Calvin Klein and Tommy Hilfiger) and specialty stores make it worth the trip.

LOCAL SHOPPING

Beyond the malls lie hundreds of unique specialty stores. From ethnic food and vintage clothing stores to electronics and book stores, there are many interesting shopping spots that escape the attention of most tourists. Here are a few highlights; for the names of more specialty stores, pick up one of the city's free newsweeklies, *Vegas Seven* (http://vegasseven.com) or *Las Vegas Weekly* (http://lasvegasweekly.com).

The Attic, tel: 702-388 4088, may be the most famous vintage store in America, owing to it featuring in both a Visa credit-card commercial and on extreme sports TV network ESPN 2. This two-story collection of clothes, appliances, and knick-knacks serves a willing audience with its selection of period clothing, often being called upon to provide items for movies being filmed in Las Vegas. Plan on spending a long time at this store, which is located at 1010 North Main Street.

Book-lovers will adore the **Gamblers Book Club**, tel: 702-382 7555, http://gamblersbookclub.com, a bookstore that specializes exclusively in – you guessed it – books about gambling. The place is renowned particularly for its poker book collection.

For souvenirs more directly associated with gambling, there is the **Gamblers' General Store**, tel: 702-382 9903, www.gamblersgeneralstore.com, a centrally located supplier of slot machines, gaming tables, and other gaming accoutrements large and small. Most items can be shipped for the purchaser if requested.

Las Vegas is one of the few North American cities that doesn't frown upon smokers. For a taste of authentic Native American tobacco, the **Paiute Tribal Smoke Shop**, tel: 702-366 1101, www.lvpaiutesmokeshop.com, sells tax-free tobacco products from its drive-through window, so you can cruise right back to the casino, light up, and lose all that money you just saved.

SPORTS

Las Vegas is a sporting city. Whether you want to watch championship boxing matches, bet on the New York Giants, go paragliding, skiing, or play 18 holes of golf, all it takes is the right toys and plenty of cash. If you engage in an outdoor sport, remember that valley temperatures can reach well above 100°F (38°C) in summer and below freezing in winter, so it's important to follow any local precautions, like using sunscreen or buying thermal underwear.

SPECTATOR SPORTS

BOXING

Las Vegas has a long boxing history, having hosted enough championship fights to qualify as a capital of the sport. A big-time bout at one of the three resorts that handle most of the action – the MGM Grand, Caesars Palace, or Mandalay Bay– invariably draws a crowd heavy with celebrities.

GOLF TOURNAMENTS

The Shriners Hospitals for Children Open held every fall at the TPC at Summerlin is considered the city's top golf attraction. Check out the PGA website at www.pgatour.com for up-to-date information, and other local golfing events.

MOTOR SPORTS

Serious racing arrived in Vegas in 1996 with the opening of the IRL Las Vegas 500 (http://www.lvms.com), 17 miles (27km) north of Downtown on Interstate 15. The 1,200-acre (490-hectare) site is a speed-fan's dream: a 1.5-mile (2.5-km) tri-oval super speedway, plus smaller clay and paved ovals, a drag strip, a road track, and a motocross course. More than 140,000 fans regularly fill the facility for NASCAR events like the Boyd Gaming 300, Whelen All-American Series, and Camping World Truck Series races.

Good for the sole

Walking the malls can be hard on the feet, just like the miles of casino aisles. For comfort, wear soft-soled shoes.

Boxer Floyd Mayweather at the MGM Grand

RODEO
Held every December, this is the largest rodeo event in the country. It's an action-packed 10-day festival of the nation's top cowboys and cowgirls riding bulls, busting broncos, and roping calves at the Thomas and Mack Center. The city goes Western with endless satellite events, like beauty pageants, parties and dances at bars, cowboy-themed art exhibits, musical events at the Fremont Street Experience, and golf tournaments. If you want to attend, plan well ahead, as last-minute tickets for the big rodeo events are hard to come by.

OTHER SPORTS
While lacking a major sports franchise, Las Vegas is home to a triple-A baseball team. The Las Vegas 51s – the city's long-est-running professional sports outfit – is a farm team for New York Mets; tickets are usually available for the Cashman Field home games.

PARTICIPATORY SPORTS

CYCLING

Although recent years have seen the construction of miles of new bike lanes and bike racks, it is better to avoid cycling on Sin City's busier streets. The best places are local parks or cycle-friendly spots beyond the city limits. One favorite, the 13-mile (21-km) scenic loop at **Red Rock Canyon**, explores some of the area's more picturesque landscapes and is not overly taxing. Free bike maps of Las Vegas and Southern Nevada can be downloaded at www.rtcsnv.com/cycling.

Mountain bikers can call **Escape Adventures**, tel: 702-596 2953, www.escapeadventures.com, to arrange a more rugged ride through the canyon's Cottonwood Valley. Another good bet: Floyd Lamb State Park, a few miles north on US95. These bike paths wind among ponds, trees, and historic buildings.

GOLF

For a desert city, Las Vegas has more than enough grass fairways and water hazards to keep the most avid duffer busy – at least 70 courses in total. Guests staying at any of the MGM Resorts hotels (which include the Mirage, MGM Grand, Bellagio, Aria, and New York-New York, to name a few) can play the spectacular **Shadow Creek** course, tel: 866-260 0069, www.shadowcreek.com; limo transport is included with all greens fees. **Angel Park Golf Club**, tel: 888-446 5358, www.angelpark.com, is a municipal course with two 18-hole courses designed by Arnold Palmer, and **Cloud Nine**, a 12-hole par-3 course featuring replicas of famous par-3 holes from around the world.

The **Las Vegas Paiute Resort**, tel: 702-658 1400, www.lvpaiutegolf.com, is 20 miles (32km) north of town but well worth the trip: one of its two courses – called Snow

Mountain – was once designated the best public course in Southern Nevada by *Golf Digest*. The Legacy Golf Club, tel: 888-629 3930, www.thelegacygc.com, in Henderson is also well respected. For a locator map and a course-by-course description, go to www.lasvegasgolf.com.

HIKING

The Las Vegas Valley is rimmed with quality hiking trails. One of the more scenic is the 5-mile (8-km) **River Mountains Trail** with fine views of Lake Mead and the valley. **Red Rock Canyon** affords numerous routes, including a 2-mile (3-km) Pine Creek Canyon trek and a slightly longer walk along the attractive Keystone Thrust Trail. **Mount Charleston** is webbed with good hikes; the ranger station can supply information, tel: 702-872 5408, http://mtcharlestonlodge.com. Another fine spot is the Valley of Fire.

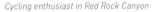

Cycling enthusiast in Red Rock Canyon

Vegas boasts at least 70 golf courses

ROCK CLIMBING

Red Rock Canyon, just 20 minutes from the Strip, has the best climbing in the region. There are literally thousands of challenges, from small bouldering routes to towering, experts-only cliffs. Spring and fall are the best seasons, but on almost any weekend there will be a cross-section of the international rock-jock community roping up in the canyon. **Red Rock Climbing Center**, tel: 702-254 5604, www.redrock climbingcenter.com, can arrange climbing trips.

SNOW SPORTS

Mount Charleston has a ski area, the **Las Vegas Ski and Snowboard Resort**, also known as Lee Canyon, tel: 702-645 2754, www.skilasvegas.com. It has bunny, intermediate, and expert routes, along with ski rental, ski school, and a lounge.

CASINOS AND KIDS

By law, people under the age of 21 are not permitted in any casino gaming areas, bars, or lounges, but some casinos are child-friendly if certain rules are followed (children must not be left unattended; children may walk through a casino when accompanied by a parent, but may not stop). Other casinos ban strollers from the premises or close the doors entirely to anyone under 18 unless they are guests staying with an adult. If you are a parent desperate for a little grown-up fun, most hotels can arrange babysitting services.

The natural snowfall is often augmented by snow-making equipment. The resort has nine long runs on 40 acres (16 hectares), but despite its name, snowboarding is allowed only at certain times.

TENNIS
A select few resorts have tennis facilities, but these are often for guests only. The main municipal tennis courts are at the **Amanda and Stacy Darling Memorial Tennis Center**, tel: 702-229 2100.

LAS VEGAS FOR CHILDREN
Although Las Vegas is now an adult town again after a decade of wooing the family market, there are still a number of kid-friendly activities. Most casinos have at least some kind of arcade, but the true high-scorer is **GameWorks**, www.gameworks.com. Highlights include an eight-lane bowling center and an eGaming Arena. If you play up an appetite, GameWorks also has a full-service restaurant and a patio for alfresco dining.

In the Showcase Mall next to the MGM Grand is **M&M's World**, four stories of merchandise and memorabilia dedicated to the famous small, round and ever-popular candies. Inside, the miles of aisles are loaded with thousands of fun M&M-related knickknacks, souvenirs, and collectibles; for sheer novelty, sample the hard-to-find silver M&Ms.

THRILLS AND SPILLS FOR OLDER KIDS
Circus Circus' **Adventuredome**, www.adventuredome.com, a climate-controlled pink dome behind the venerable hotel-casino, boasts attractions including the Canyon Blaster corkscrew roller coaster, a water ride, bumper cars, carnival games, and a laser tag arena. The casino itself features kid-friendly free circus acts from 11am to midnight daily.

Roller-coaster aficionados will love the twisting, looping **Big Apple Coaster** at New York-New York. Once inside the hotel, stop at the extensive Coney Island-themed arcade. Ultra high-altitude thrills are the order of the day at the Stratosphere Tower. The **Big Shot** slingshot ride heightens the sensation of sudden vertical acceleration with its setting 1,100ft (335m) above the city, while **X-Scream** takes riders with stomachs of iron almost as high, then dangles them in the air.

Plenty of places for kids to explore

FURTHER AFIELD

Even farther from the bright lights is **Bonnie Springs Ranch**, tel: 702-875 4191, https://bonniesprings.com, a mock ghost town near Red Rock Canyon. The Wild-West town comes complete with gunfights, a wax museum, an opera house, a mini-train, horseback riding, and an extensive petting zoo.

For motorized thrills, the **Las Vegas Mini Grand Prix**, tel: 702-259 7000, www.lvmgp.com, has the West's only banked-oval stock car track. Along with go-karts and kiddie karts, the 7-acre (3-hectare) facility provides wheels for big drivers, too.

Northwest of Henderson is the factory of **Ethel M. Chocolates**, tel: 800-438 4356, www.ethelm.com, where self-guided tours are available Mon–Thu 10am–4.30pm.

CALENDAR OF EVENTS

January *The Super Bowl:* The biggest sports-betting day of the year; Sports Books are packed with anxious betters watching the game on giant TV screens. *AVN Adult Entertainment Expo:* A four-day adult entertainment trade show held annually at the Hard Rock Hotel and Casino, embracing business, stars and lots of very enthusiastic fans.

February *Chinese New Year:* The biggest gambling day of the year.

April *Vegas Uncork'd:* This up-and-coming culinary festival features numerous celebrity chefs and master sommeliers, http://vegasuncorked.com.

May *Helldorado Days:* A four-day rodeo, plus western parties and a parade celebrating Southern Nevada's cowpoke roots, www.elkshelldorado.com.

June *Electric Daisy Carnival:* electronic dance music festival, http://lasvegas.electricdaisycarnival.com.

August *Best in the Desert:* The longest off-road race in the United States starts in Las Vegas and finishes in Reno in Northern Nevada, http://bitd.com. *Las Vegas Film Festival:* The program ranges from short film showcases to feature indies, http://lvff.com.

September *Las Vegas Pride Night Parade and Festival:* A glamorous spectacle created by Las Vegas's LGBT community, http://lasvegaspride.org.

October *Shriners Hospitals for Children Open:* This golf tournament from the Tournament Players Club in Summerlin is a major event on the United States' golfing calendar, www.shrinershospitalsforchildren.org. *Life is Beautiful:* features some of the hottest music acts as well as food from top chefs, http://lifeisbeautiful.com.

November *Rock 'n' Roll Las Vegas Marathon and Half Marathon:* One of the oldest marathons in the US, now more of a pop culture phenomenon, held at night around the Strip, www.runrocknroll.com/las-vegas.

December *New Year's Eve:* Celebrate with 200,000 or more of your newest friends. Las Vegas's celebrations and the two major block parties that accompany them are challenging Times Square for attendees. Make your reservations early and come prepared to party.

EATING OUT

Dining in Las Vegas has been transformed. The wall-to-wall all-you-can-eat buffets have been sidelined, the celebrity chefs are here, and the standards and the stakes have been raised all round. Although the high-ticket gastrodomes may not be perfect for every meal, they have definitely raised the culinary game. Prices in these eateries have nearly caught up with their New York, Los Angeles, and San Franciscan cousins, but so, too, has the food and the service.

Catering at the more down-to-earth kitchens has become more expensive too, but the food is a lot better than the curling buffet fare of yesterday. Sitting side-by-side with the paying customers are a new breed; gamblers are regularly rewarded for their play by pit bosses scribbling out comps (complimentary tickets) for the hotel's on-site restaurants. The level of the comp depends upon the level of play, so everyone – low-rollers to big spenders – can be accommodated. And what could be better than a free meal in Las Vegas?

CELEBRITY CHEFS

Wolfgang Puck started it all in 1992 when he opened a second location of his ultra-chic Hollywood restaurant, Spago, in Caesars Palace. Six years later, hotelier Steve Wynn set the standard for casino resorts by hiring three of America's top chefs, Michael Mina, Todd English, and Jean-George Vongerichten, to run restaurants in the Bellagio. Today, every major resort has at least one extravagant restaurant where you need reservations weeks in advance. Award-winning chefs often name restaurants after themselves. You'll find Barmasa (named after Masa Takayama) in Aria, Bradley Ogden in Caesars, and Joël Robuchon in the MGM Grand. As for Wolfgang Puck, he now has six fine-dining restaurants on the Las Vegas Strip.

CUISINES OF THE WORLD

With the arrival of Wolfgang Puck's Spago in 1992, the city began a slow but sure ascent from the depths of continental cuisine into the modern world of the nouvelle, haute, California, Pan Asian, and Pacific Rim. Since then, more star chefs have brought their operations to Las Vegas, among them Emeril Lagasse and Joël Robuchon.

Carnivores won't go wrong in Vegas

NEW ON THE MENU

Acting in concert with these arrivals was the hotels' new-found willingness to relinquish ownership and management of some of their dining spaces to experienced restaurateurs. The result for food lovers has been terrific. The improvement of the dining experience and the resulting rise of expectations led to an across-the-board renewal. Today, some of the city's – and even the country's – best restaurants are ensconced within hotel-casinos, such as Picasso at Bellagio, Carnevino at the Palazzo, Twist at the Mandarin Oriental, and RM Seafood at Mandalay Bay.

BOUNTIFUL BUFFETS

Despite these changes to the culinary landscape, buffets can still be a hit-and-miss affair, with many offering similar selections of prime rib, starchy vegetables, limp salads, and boring desserts. Others offer a wide array of cuisines – Mexican, Italian, American heartland (in other words, meat and potatoes), and vegetables – plus all the seconds, thirds,

'Al fresco' dining at New York-New York

and fourths you can handle. Truly adventurous eaters will love the Buffet of Buffets at Caesars properties; a pass starting from $54.99 gets diners 24 hours of unlimited access to six different buffets across five different properties.

Generally speaking, the Rio's Carnival World Buffet is definitely a cut above, as is the Buffet at Wynn, inside Wynn Las Vegas. All buffets, regardless of class, status, price, or time of day or night, have lines that stretch around the block. Expect to pay for a buffet before you enter. Once inside, you can eat all you wish, though it is considered unacceptable to bring food out of the buffet area. Soft drinks are often included in the price of the buffet, but beer and wine is purchased separately at the register.

CHAMPAGNE BRUNCH

Sunday Champagne brunches were once the best of the buffets, despite champagne that was not always palatable. Today, most are simply a more expensive version of the standard breakfast-lunch offerings. Bally's Sterling Brunch is a notable exception. Replete with ice sculptures and fresh flowers, it is a spread fit for a king (but it is also expensive).

THEME RESTAURANTS

Theme restaurants have proliferated in Las Vegas. Local versions of the Hard Rock Café and the Harley Davidson Café pull the same brisk business that they do around the globe. Chain franchises from fast food to pancake houses are now sucking up much of the local dining budget. But when the population of Vegas skyrocketed in the middle of the last decade, more upscale chains also made their way to the valley. As a result, locally-owned dining is also experiencing a boom, and many ethnic and specialty restaurants have opened.

HOME-GROWN TALENT

A growing restaurant row has evolved along Paradise Road, where diners can choose from a plethora of major restaurants, locally-owned eateries, and ethnic cafés, all within walking distance of each another. Chinatown, near Spring Mountain Road, is another good place to check out, offering excellent cuisine that includes Filipino and Vietnamese, as well as the more common Chinese.

Gourmet chocolates

In fact, considering how rapidly the dining situation has improved – and the truckloads of money being spent to lure world-class chefs – Las Vegas may someday overtake all of its American rivals in the culinary sweepstakes.

PLACES TO EAT

Price ranges are per person for a typical main course. A large tip of 15–20 percent is appropriate, and often expected.

$$$$ $30 and over   **$$$** $25–$30
$$ $13–$24   **$** under $12

STRIP RESTAURANTS

Barmasa $$$–$$$$ *Aria Las Vegas, tel: 877-230 2742, www.aria laslasvegas.com.* Dinner only. This elegant and modern eatery features a vaulted ceiling and natural elements such as stone and running water. Fish is flown in daily from all over the world, making the sushi second to none.

Blue Ribbon Sushi Bar & Grill $$$$ *The Cosmopolitan of Las Vegas, tel: 877-893 2003, www.cosmopolitanlasvegas.com.* Dinner only. The Vegas outpost of this famous New York eatery serves up much more than just sushi; the fried chicken with wasabi honey is, without question, the best fried chicken you'll ever eat.

Carnevino $$$$ *The Palazzo Resort Hotel Casino, tel: 702-789 4141, www.palazzo.com.* Dinner only. Chef Mario Batali and winemaker Joe Bastianich have teamed up for a number of restaurants inside the Venetian and Palazzo, but this authentic Italian steakhouse (with a wine list featuring Italian wines) is one of the best.

Joël Robuchon $$$$ *MGM Grand Hotel & Casino, tel: 702-891 7925, www.mgmgrand.com.* Dinner only. Meals are works of art at this ultra high-end restaurant, where the prix-fixe, multi-course meals take four hours to consume. Just be sure you bring the cash; some of the tasting menus cost upward of $500.

Mastro's Ocean Club $$$$ *Crystals (inside City Center), tel: 702-798 7115, www.theshopsatcrystals.com.* Dinner only. Sure, the fish at this restaurant is delicious, but the real attraction is the restaurant itself; the eatery sits in a two-story wooden sculpture dubbed 'The Treehouse.' It's a great place to see and be seen.

Mon Ami Gabi $–$$$ *Paris Las Vegas, tel: 702-944 4224*, www. monamigabi.com. Breakfast, lunch, and dinner. Enjoy the passing crowds from this raised café backed by a facade of the Louvre, and the lake show across the street. Order classic steak frites or the fruits de mer. On weekends, try the brunch.

Picasso $$$$ *Bellagio, tel: 702-693 8865*, www.bellagio.com. Open Wed–Mon dinner only. The French cooking of master chef Julian Serrano has ensured that Picasso is now a restaurant of national importance. While you're waiting for the next culinary treat, admire the art on the walls. They really are by that other, even more famous, master.

Rainforest Café $$ *MGM Grand Hotel and Casino, tel: 702-891 8580*, www.mgmgrand.com. Breakfast, lunch, and dinner. Kids love this loud, family-style restaurant with its lush jungle environment, life-size animatronic beasts, and simulated thunderstorms. The entrance is through an arched aquarium. The menu offers standard American fare under exotic names.

RM Seafood $$$–$$$$ *Mandalay Bay Resort and Casino, tel: 702-632 9300*, www.rmseafood.com. Lunch and dinner. Rick Moonen's homage to fish is two restaurants in one – a casual downstairs featuring sushi and a raw bar, and a more formal upstairs with a multi-course chef's tasting menu. All ingredients are sustainably harvested.

Spago $$$ *The Forum Shops, tel: 702-369 6300*, www.caesars.com, www.wolfgangpuck.com. Lunch and dinner. One of the first Los Angeles eateries to introduce fusion cooking techniques, Wolfgang Puck's Las Vegas restaurant is as much about being seen as it is about eating. A French-, Asian-, and Italian-inspired menu ends with fabulous desserts.

Stack $$$–$$$$ *The Mirage, tel: 866-339 4566*, www.mirage.com, http://stacklasvegas.com. Dinner only. Wooden walls welcome diners to this hip and happening restaurant, which serves American classics with a contemporary twist. Be sure to try the Adult Tater Tots with bacon and brie.

SW Steakhouse $$$$ *Encore, tel: 877-321 9966*, www.wynnlas vegas.com. Dinner only. Chef David Walzog cooks an outstanding

American steakhouse fare, including great steaks. For the weight watchers, the menu has lower-calorie versions of some of the most popular dishes.

Top of the World $$$$ *Stratosphere Casino, Hotel and Tower,* tel: *702-380 7711,* www.stratospherehotel.com. Lunch and dinner. The food often takes second place here, as the revolving restaurant offers a full-circle view of Vegas every hour. Though the view is unparalleled, the continental cuisine is not bad.

Twist $$$$ *Mandarin Oriental Las Vegas,* tel: *888-881 9367,* www.mandarinoriental.com/lasvegas. Dinner only. Elaborate prix-fixe, multi-course meals feature the fusion style that Chef Pierre Gagnaire has made famous. The setting is spectacular, too; the restaurant looks out over Vegas on the Mandarin's 23rd floor.

Wing Lei $$$–$$$$ *Wynn Las Vegas,* tel: *702-248-3463,* www.wynnlasvegas.com. Dinner only. Chinese food goes upscale at this beautiful eatery, which serves up a blend of Cantonese, Szechuan, and Shanghai cooking styles. Peking duck, a house specialty, is worth the wait.

DOWNTOWN RESTAURANTS

Hugo's Cellar $$$ *Four Queens Hotel and Casino,* tel: *702-385 4011,* http://hugoscellar.com. Dinner only. An excellent wine list complements this unexpected Downtown gem. The continental cuisine is a bit dated, but the experience is elegant and romantic.

Luv-It Frozen Custard $ *505 East Oakley Boulevard,* tel: *702-384 6452,* www.luvitfrozencustard.com. Dessert only. Frozen custard is the only item on the menu at this legendary spot near the Stratosphere. It's similar to soft-serve ice cream, only creamier.

Top of Binion's Steakhouse $$$–$$$$ *Binion's Gambling Hall,* tel: *702-382 1600,* www.binions.com. Dinner only. Some of the best beef in the West comes through this steakhouse. The long-time owners, the Binions, were ranchers as well as casino-owners. Great 24th-floor view of the city.

Triple 7 Restaurant and Microbrewery $ *Main Street Station Casino, Brewery and Hotel, tel: 702-387 1896,* www.mainstreetcasino.com. Lunch and dinner. Ales and beers brewed on the premises complement a fresh and innovative menu of American and Asian cuisine, as well as delicious wood-fired pizzas.

Vic & Anthony's $$–$$$$ *Golden Nugget Hotel, tel: 702-386 8399,* www.vicandanthonys.com. Dinner only. Succulent beef, tender lobster, and more highlight the menu at this dark, intimate steakhouse. It's a great place for a business meal.

OFF-STRIP RESTAURANTS

35 Steaks + Martinis $$$–$$$$ *Hard Rock Hotel and Casino, tel: 702-693 5500,* www.hardrockhotel.com. Dinner only. Cutting-edge cocktails and steak aged 35 days (hence the name) are among the highlights at the Hard Rock's newest steakhouse. Naturally, the wine list features Pink Floyd and Led Zeppelin labels.

Carnival World Buffet $$$–$$$$ *Rio All-Suite Hotel and Casino, tel: 702-777 7757,* www.caesars.com. Brunch, lunch, and dinner. The main attractions here are the numerous cooked-to-order food stations ranging from Asian to Mexican to Italian. The buffet combines a fresh-food approach with the mass-audience aesthetic.

Chicago Joe's $–$$ *820 South 4th Street, tel: 702-382 5637,* http://chicagojoesrestaurant.com. Lunch and dinner. Closed Sun–Mon. A tiny restaurant in a former Downtown home, Joe's has been serving tasty southern Italian pastas and shellfish for more than 30 years.

Golden Steer Steakhouse $$$ *308 West Sahara Avenue, tel: 702-384 4470,* http://goldensteersteakhouselasvegas.com. The Golden Steer is one of the classic Vegas steakhouses, with an atmosphere of a bordello. If you like big steaks served in dark booths, you'll love this place.

Hofbräuhaus $$ *4510 Paradise Road, tel: 702-853 2337,* www.hofbrauhauslasvegas.com. Lunch and dinner. A replica of Munich's famous brewery, this huge restaurant across the street from the

Hard Rock Hotel serves traditional Bavarian cuisine in a cheery Oktoberfest atmosphere.

Lindo Michoacan $$ *2655 East Desert Inn Road, tel: 702-735 6828,* www.lindomichoacan.com. Lunch and dinner. This authentic Mexican restaurant serves elaborate south-of-the-border cuisine. Specialties include roasted goat meat that is served with rich sauces and freshly-made flour tortillas.

Lotus of Siam $–$$$ *953 East Sahara Avenue, tel: 702-735 3033,* www.saipinchutima.com. Lunch and dinner. Chef Saipin Chutima serves up northern-style Thai Food at this tiny restaurant, deemed by many to be the best Thai eatery in the US. Regulars swear by the Drunken Noodles.

Marche Bacchus $$–$$$$ *2620 Regatta Drive, tel: 702-804 8008,* http://marchebacchus.com. Lunch and dinner. When Strip chefs go out for meals in the Vegas suburbs, most come to this French Bistro on the shores of Lake Las Vegas. Wine is imported from France; much of it is available in the adjacent wine market.

Marssa $$–$$$$ *101 Montelago Boulevard, tel: 702-567 6125,* www. marssalasvegas.com. Lunch and dinner. Sushi and Asian-fusion cuisine dominate the menu at this bright and airy eatery overlooking Lake Las Vegas at the Westin Lake Las Vegas resort.

Nora's Cuisine $$–$$$ *6020 West Flamingo Road, tel: 702-873 8990,* www.norascuisine.com. Lunch and dinner. Authentic Sicilian food is the specialty at this cozy family-owned restaurant just off the Strip.

Paymon's Mediterranean Café $$ *4147 South Maryland Parkway, tel: 702-731 6030,* http://paymons.com. Lunch and dinner. With its tantalizing menu of Greek, Middle Eastern, and Persian food, this deli-style eatery has been a local favorite for more than 20 years. It's one of the best places in town for vegetarian fare.

Ruth's Chris Steak House $$$ *Harrah's Casino Las Vegas, 3475 Las Vegas Boulevard South, tel: 702-693-6000,* www.ruthschris.com. Lunch and dinner daily. Ruth Fertel opened her first restaurant in New Orleans in 1965; now her tasty steaks can be ordered all over the US.

A–Z TRAVEL TIPS

A Summary of Practical Information

A

ACCOMMODATIONS (See also Camping, Youth Hostels, and the list of Recommended Hotels starting on page 132)

Las Vegas is a unique city in that the vast majority of its hotels offer both accommodations and attractions. Most of the places travelers want to see are found along the Strip or Downtown, so staying in one of these areas will put you right in the center of the action.

The quality of accommodations ranges from the sleaziest to the best, but most of the **hotel-casinos** fall comfortably into the average to above-average categories. Off-Strip hotel-casinos offer many of the same amenities – and sometimes more – as on-Strip hotels, and often at a lower price. Neighborhood hotel-casinos usually offer less in the way of amenities, but make up for it in price.

There are **non-gaming resorts** (such as the Mandarin Oriental and the Four Seasons) if you prefer classy accommodations away from the clang of slot machines. Also, there are **non-gaming motels** all over the city, in the suburbs, and along Boulder Highway. Many of them specialize in extended stays of a week or more, and can be good alternatives for travelers on a budget.

If you will be without a car, choose a hotel as close to your preferred action as possible. Las Vegas sprawls, taxis are costly, and public transportation is still getting up to speed.

As there is no truly slow season in Las Vegas, room reservations are strongly advised, especially during the heavy travel periods in fall and spring and on any weekend, during major sporting events, for New Year's Eve, and whenever there is a major trade convention in town. In fact, some of the conventions draw more than 200,000 people – enough to fill almost every room in the city. The **Las Vegas Convention and Visitors**

Authority, tel: 702-892 0711, www.lvcva.com, can alert you to when there is an event in town. Alternatively, search the LVCVA website at www.visitlasvegas.com for availability, or visit another Vegas website such as www.vegas.com.

There are still periods of relative quiet when rates are down and it is easier to find a room without reservations. The city is usually slower between Thanksgiving (fourth Thursday of November) and Christmas, as well as during the high-heat months of July and August. Then, room rates are up for grabs, and incredible bargains can be found. If you're feeling brave, it's always worth negotiating. You could, for example, book a room on-line for the first couple of nights, then simply stroll from one resort to the next, asking for the best rate on that particular day.

AIRPORT

Las Vegas is served by one major airport, **McCarran International** (tel: 702-261 5211, www.mccarran.com). With the growth in travel to Las Vegas, the airport is among the country's busiest. The airport is also very close to town, within a 15-minute drive of Tropicana Avenue and the Strip. Transportation to and from the airport is available via an unending stream of taxis (though wait times can sometimes exceed one hour).

For a cheaper ride, try one of the shuttle buses that operate 24 hours and take you directly to your hotel. Two of such companies are is **Bell Trans** (tel: 800-274 7433, www.bell-trans.com) and Airline Shuttle (tel: 702-444 1234, www.bestairlineshuttle.com); they offer pre-arranged limousines, too. A public bus serves the airport, but it takes far longer than the relatively inexpensive shuttle buses.

If you'd like to explore Las Vegas by public transportation, the 109-Maryland Parkway bus serves McCarran Airport and the South Strip Transport Center, where you can change to a bus serving the Strip, Downtown, or other destinations.

B

BICYCLE RENTAL

Bicycle riding within the Strip area is not advised; the streets are not designed for cycling, and the drivers are not used to sharing the road, although the city has become more bicycle-friendly in recent years. Free bike maps of Las Vegas and Southern Nevada can be downloaded at www.rtcsnv.com/cycling. For bicycle rental and tours of the surrounding natural areas by bicycle, call **Escape Adventures** on 702-596 2953, www.escapeadventures. com.

BUDGETING FOR YOUR TRIP

Las Vegas is one of the less expensive vacation destinations in the US – if you stay away from the tables. Once a flight has been paid for, everything else can be done on the cheap, from dining at a $7.99 buffet, to staying in a decent motel for as little as $25 per night. Sin City is a place that likes to do deals, and car rental firms and even major casinos often offer astonishingly low prices, usually in the summer months of July and August. If money is tight, it's worth deciding in advance when you want to go, and shopping around on the Internet for competitive offers. Of course, it's also possible to spend a fortune in Vegas, especially if you take advantage of all the shopping and show opportunities; top shows like Cirque du Soleil can cost up to $150 per ticket. Museums and attractions charge hefty admission prices, too, often around $20.

The best way to blow your budget is to gamble. Setting and holding yourself to a daily limit is a good strategy for keeping control of the cash. Decide before leaving home exactly how much per day you have for gambling and do not permit yourself to exceed that amount; access to bank accounts via debit cards is far too easy, and many only dole out $100 bills. More than a few travelers have arrived here happy, only to be forced to sell a prized possession for the fare home.

Tipping must be budgeted for as well. It is a recognized and accepted part of Las Vegas culture, and being unprepared can result in poor service (see Tipping).

C

CAMPING

Within the city limits, there are plenty of RV parks, for example behind Circus Circus that has 170 RV sites and free Wi-fi. Other parks include KOA (tel: 702-454 8055, http://koa.com) at Sam's Town on Boulder Highway.

Outside of the city, camping is plentiful in Red Rock Canyon, the Valley of Fire, and Mount Charleston, with Red Rock being only 30 minutes from the city (see Excursions, page 63).

CAR RENTAL

If you're planning to leave the Strip, Downtown, or the immediate vicinity of your hotel, you should consider renting a car. Most do so at the centralized, off-site airport location accessible by free shuttle bus from all terminals. Advance reservations are suggested but not required. Most of the major US companies are represented (Alamo, Avis, Budget, Dollar, Enterprise, Hertz, National, and Thrifty), and rates are generally below the US average. Many major companies usually won't rent to drivers under 25 years of age, but some of the local companies will. All rental companies require a driver's license and a major credit card matching the license. Price quotes do not include taxes or liability and collision damage waivers (CDW). These can double the cost, so check with your credit card company to see what is already covered. No added insurance is required, but renters should weigh that choice carefully, since Las Vegas traffic can be aggressive.

CLIMATE

Las Vegas is a desert region, making summer temperatures very warm and dry and winters cold. August temperatures can reach over 115°F (46°C) in the mid-afternoon, and still hover around 100°F (38°C) at midnight. Winter temperatures can be surprisingly brisk at noon, reaching 58°F (14°C), and dipping very quickly after the sun sets, to 34°F (1°C). Spring is warmer but windy; fall is often the best time to visit, with warm days and mild nights. The sun shines an average of 310 days per year, so bring sunglasses and leave the umbrella at home.

	J	F	M	A	M	J	J	A	S	O	N	D
High												
°F	47	50	55	63	73	83	90	87	80	67	53	45
°C	8	10	13	17	23	28	32	31	27	19	17	7
Low												
°F	33	37	42	49	59	68	75	73	65	53	41	33
°C	0	3	6	9	15	20	24	23	18	17	7	0

CLOTHING

Requirements for dressing in Las Vegas have fluctuated over the years, from the formality of the 1940s through the 1960s to the T-shirts and shorts of the 1990s. Today's styles range from upscale sumptuous to downright shoddy, with everything imaginable in between. Little is out of place here, though remember that many of the better restaurants require jackets and ties for men.

Remember also to pack clothing appropriate for the weather; short sleeves and skirts or shorts are accepted and nearly required for spending time outside in the summer months. Heavy winter jackets are what most winter visitors forget to pack, not expecting the chill of the winds that frequently assail the city. Sunblock is a must; a style-appropriate hat, or at least a pair of sunglasses, is highly recommended.

CRIME AND SAFETY

Las Vegas is a fairly safe place considering the high volume of tourist traffic. Hotel security is notoriously efficient (look up; the black-glass bubbles on the ceilings are a marker of security cameras monitored 24 hours a day), and Metro police bicycle patrols help curb problems along the Strip and Downtown. Still, standard big-city precautions should be taken. Avoid dark areas, especially in Downtown. Pick-pocketing in crowded areas – such as the Bellagio's fountain display – is notorious, so watch your suitcases, purse, or wallet. In any emergency, dial 911 from any phone; no coins needed.

Visitors are much more likely to become a victim of an accident than a crime. Tourists walking down the Strip often become distracted by all the visual stimuli, so much so that it's not uncommon for people to walk into oncoming traffic. In many cases, the pedestrians are at fault, meandering into streets while looking at the lights, foolishly crossing the Strip's eight lanes of bumper-to-bumper traffic between lights, or simply backing into a lane of traffic while angling for a photograph. When walking in Las Vegas it is crucial to remember that, despite the temptation, you must not jaywalk or hop over barricades meant to prohibit pedestrian travel. Motorists are notoriously possessive of their travel lanes, and laws are set against pedestrians that violate the travel lane beyond a crosswalk.

D

DRIVING

Driving can be a difficult experience for anyone unused to city traffic. Las Vegas streets are busy and the drivers aggressive and unpredictable. Roads that are complete are in very good condition, owing to recent widening and paving, but there are many roadways under perpetual expansion and construction.

A right turn on a red light is permitted in Vegas, unless otherwise posted. U-turns are allowed, as well. When a stoplight turns green, be sure to check both directions before proceeding; Las Vegans are notorious for their attempts (and failures) to beat the traffic signal. Watch for school-crossing zones; fines are high and local patrols are often on watch. However tempting, never drink and drive, as penalties are stiff and can include an immediate period in jail.

Freeways are the I-15 traveling north from Los Angeles to Salt Lake City, and US93/95, which comes from Arizona toward Utah. Interstate 215 connects the Strip and airport with the booming suburbs of Henderson and Summerlin.

Parking is easy, with every hotel offering free parking lots or structures. Valet parking is a free at-the-door service, but tips are customary. Remember that on busy nights, the valet may take longer to retrieve your car than you could have if you parked yourself *(see Tipping)*. Also, valets are not responsible for damages.

Gasoline is plentiful, available on nearly every corner and, though expensive by US standards, inexpensive compared to elsewhere in the world, especially Europe.

E

ELECTRICITY

All of the United States uses a 110-120 volt 50-cycle alternating current (AC). Transformers or plug adaptors are required for appliances using any other voltage, and are widely available.

EMERGENCIES

Dial **911** from any phone, toll-free.

G

GAY AND LESBIAN TRAVELERS

While Las Vegas may have a reputation as Sin City, it is only quietly tolerant of its fairly large gay and lesbian community, in the same look-the-other-way manner in which many gay entertainers have been accepted. Many gay businesses, bars, and nightclubs are centered in the small, energetic Fruit Loop, an area off Paradise Road between Harmon and Tropicana. For information and good listings, pick up *Q-Vegas* magazine (www.qvegas.com), available at most major record and bookstores.

GETTING THERE (see also Airport and Driving)

There are only three modern methods of transportation available for passengers coming to Las Vegas: air, bus, or car.

By air. Las Vegas, though a major travel destination, is still considered a second-tier city when it comes to direct flights. While most major US cities, especially in the West, offer direct flights into McCarran International (the city's only major airport), many East Coast cities use hubs such as Denver, Chicago, and Phoenix. While some airlines add new direct flights on occasion, others withdraw theirs. Direct, international flights come from Frankfurt, London, Mexico City, and many Canadian cities. Call the **Las Vegas Convention and Visitors Authority** at 702-892 0711 for information about international direct flights; call your airline regarding other flights.

By bus. Greyhound Bus Lines offers daily bus travel to and from Las Vegas and surrounding cities. Call 1-800-231 2222 (toll-free in the US) for information, www.greyhound.com.

By car. *See Driving.*

GUIDES AND TOURS

Numerous tour operators are located in Las Vegas, and their advertisements can be found in almost every free guide available along the Strip. The majority specialize in tours of Southern Nevada's Lake Mead (where you can also take a high-speed boat or a dinner cruise); to Hoover Dam and Boulder City; or to Red

Rock Canyon. One of the most exciting excursions, which can be done by bus, plane, or mostly glamorously of all, by helicopter, is to the Grand Canyon (see page 92). This round-trip journey can be done in under a day, returning to Sin City just in time to have a shower, a late dinner, and still give you time to hit the casinos that evening.

(see page 92)

H

HEALTH AND MEDICAL CARE

Las Vegas is a modern city with modern health care and food standards. In the event of an emergency, there are six area hospitals that provide 24-hour emergency care. Travelers needing medical attention in a non-emergency situation should seek out a **University Medical Center Quick Care** clinic (tel: 702-383 CARE); go to: www.umcsn.com for a map. These centers require no appointments, and accept most patients, but be prepared to wait up to an hour or two. If you have no health insurance (or your insurance is not recognized), you will have to pay for medical services immediately, so be sure to ask in advance about payment procedures.

Complementing this, there are several pharmacies for prescription and non-prescription drugs. **Walgreens** (www.walgreens.com) has over a dozen locations; most are open 24 hours daily.

HOLIDAYS

Most businesses' opening hours are similar to public holidays. Hotel-casinos and resorts never close, regardless of the day or time, but grocery stores keep shorter hours on Christmas and Thanksgiving (fourth Thursday of November). Government offices, schools, the post office, and banks are closed for national holidays. Holiday times are extremely busy at Las Vegas airport. The Fourth of July and New Year's Eve holidays really attract the crowds, with Christmas following closely behind. Though not an

fficial holiday in the US, Chinese New Year is a busy holiday in
as Vegas casinos, too.

MEDIA

Las Vegas has two daily **newspapers**: the *Review-Journal* (www.
reviewjournal.com) and the *Las Vegas Sun* (http://lasvegassun.
com). The *Review-Journal* has a more national orientation, while
the *Sun* reads like the local metropolitan daily that it has always
been. Hotel news-stands carry both, as well as the *The New York
Times*, *Los Angeles Times*, *USA Today*, and the *Wall Street Journal*.

There are a dozen **free local tourist guides**, ranging from small
booklets of ads to more elaborate magazines with information content and listings. Two are *What's On: The Las Vegas Guide* (http://
whats-on.com) and *Las Vegas Magazine* (http://lasvegasmagazine.
com). *What's On* is available in most hotel lobbies and on news racks,
while Las Vegas magazine is found in hotel rooms throughout the city.

Las Vegas also has two **free alternative newsweeklies**, *Vegas
Seven* (http://vegasseven.com) and the *Las Vegas Weekly* (http://las
vegasweekly.com). They are available citywide in coffeehouses, cafés,
bookstores, clubs, bars, and newspaper racks, and contain extensive
listings of off-Strip information.

The valley's **television** is primarily served by Cox Communications
cable system, with almost 100 channels. Most hotel rooms have at
least these stations: MTV, CNN, and USA networks, plus local affili-
ates ABC (channel 13), CBS (channel 8), FOX (channel 5), NBC (channel
3), and PBS (channel 10), though even the best hotels may not offer
premium channels such as HBO – they'd prefer you to gamble rather
than watch TV.

Radio has a full dial on both AM and FM bands. Highlights are KNPR
(88.9FM NPR news, 89.7FM classical, http://knpr.org), KUNV (91.5FM,
jazz, http://kunv.org), KOMP (92.3FM, rock, www.komp.com), KWNR

(95.5FM, country-western, www.955thebull.com), KXPT (97.1FM, classic and soft rock, www.point97.com); KXTE (107.5FM, alternative rock
http://x1075lasvegas.cbslocal.com), KDWN (720AM, talk, http://kdwr
com), and KNUU (970AM, news).

MONEY

Currency. The monetary unit in the US, the dollar, is based on the
decimal system, with 100 cents per dollar.

Common banknotes are in the $1, $5, $10, $20, $50, and $100
denominations. If you are unfamiliar with dollars, be careful han-
dling them. The bills are all the same size and color, and the denominations can be hard to distinguish in low light. Mistakes can
be costly. There are also silver dollar coins (and, in rare instances
$2 bills).

Currency exchange. While banks and other financial offices will
exchange currency, there is no need; major casino cages will do
so immediately and without commission. This is the first and best
choice for exchanging cash.

Credit cards. It's a good idea to carry at least one major credit
card with you while in Las Vegas. With the advent of checking-
based debit cards, their acceptance in stores, restaurants, and bars
is nearly universal. You will, however, still need some cash for tipping (see Tipping), as well as for the slot machines.

Travelers' checks. Travelers' checks are accepted almost
everywhere, though their relative complexity compared to credit
cards makes them best for transporting cash between home and
the casino cage, which will convert them into American currency
as you require. You need to present your passport to exchange
them for cash.

ATMs are accessible throughout all major casinos. Beware
of additional service fees – often up to $3; these will be listed
on the ATM itself. (Your bank may charge more fees on top of
these.)

Taxes. Taxation in Nevada is generally low in comparison to other US cities, thanks to heavy taxes on gaming revenue. Sales tax on merchandise and restaurant food is 6.85 percent; food (groceries) purchased in stores is exempt from sales tax. Lodging taxes are 12 percent. In addition, many hotels assess 'resort fees' to offset rising energy costs (or, simply, to make more cash).

O

OPENING HOURS

Las Vegas is a 24-hour town. The hotel-casinos and most of the city's bars never close. Though all casinos have at least one 24-hour coffee shop, most restaurants keep shorter hours, closing by 11pm on weeknights, and midnight or even 1am on Saturday and Sunday. Retail stores and malls, both on- and off-Strip, open between 9 and 10am, closing at about 9pm (although some 'destination shopping centers,' like the Forum Shops and Crystals, stay open until midnight). Grocery stores and many drugstores are open 24 hours.

P

POLICE (see also Crime and Safety)

With more than 2 million residents in the Las Vegas metropolitan area and nearly 40 million visitors annually, Las Vegas police take their work very seriously. They are generally helpful, and will guide tourists in the right direction if asked. Due to traffic problems, however, they are unusually strict about jaywalking, so pedestrians should take care to observe signs, lights, and directions. Casually uniformed bicycle patrols on the Strip and downtown have helped improve the public face of the LVPD. Call 911 in an emergency.

POST OFFICES

Local post offices are open 8.30am–5pm weekdays and, in some cases, 9am–1pm on Saturdays. There is one at 201 Las Vegas Boulevard South (Mon–Fri 9am–5pm); use the branch at 1800 North Martin Luther King Boulevard if you need longer opening hours (Mon–Fri 8.30am–5pm; Sat 9am–3pm). For more locations visit www.usps.com.

PUBLIC TRANSPORTATION

The primary public transportation system in Las Vegas is the bus system run by the Regional Transportation Commission of Southern Nevada (RTC). One of the more intensely used bus systems in the United States, the RTC network operates 24/7 (to match the casino culture) and serves much of the region.

There are two main routes of interest to visitors that are specially branded services for the resort area. The Deuce on the Strip using double-decker buses that provide a great view of the Strip operates every 15 minutes all day and every 20 minutes during the night along the Strip between the south end and downtown, serving all of the Strip resorts (including the Stratosphere) as well as the Fremont Street Experience and the Bonnevile Transit Center downtown.

The Strip and Downtown Express route operates along a similar route with long high-capacity buses making limited stops (from 9am until midnight every day, every 15 minutes) between the South Strip Transfer Center and the Grand Central Parkway area west of downtown Las Vegas, via the Strip and the Convention Center.

For these routes, a premium fare of $6 is charged (for a two-hour pass), with a 24-hour pass available for $8 and a three-day pass for $20. Note that all other bus routes in the city are cheaper, with a $2 single-ride fare, $3 for a two-hour pass, and $5 for 24 hours. One other route that may be particularly useful to visitors is 109-Maryland Parkway, which serves McCarran

Airport as well as the South Strip Transfer Center (where you can connect to buses serving the Strip) and downtown's Bonneville Transit Center. For more information about these services, see www.rtcsnv.com.

The Las Vegas Monorail (www.lvmonorail.com) is a 3.9-mile (6.3-km) monorail line that runs parallel to the Strip but to the east behind the casino resorts. There are seven stations, from MGM-Grand Station in the south (near Tropicana Avenue) to Sahara Station in the north (near Sahara Avenue), with an important station at the Las Vegas Convention Center along the route. Trains operate from 7am–2am (Mon until midnight, Fri–Sun until 3am) every 4–12 minutes, depending on the time of day, and it takes just under 15 minutes to travel from end to end. Single-ride tickets are $5, with one-day passes available for $12 and three-day passes available for $28.

Note that there are also much shorter people-mover systems that link specific resorts for free (usually those owned by the same company) – the Mandalay Bay Tram connecting Mandalay Bay, Luxor, and Excalibur; the CityCenter Tram connecting Monte Carlo, CityCenter, and Bellagio; and a tram connecting Mirage and Treasure Island. While these are not very useful for general transportation, they can help you get between certain resorts more quickly and comfortably.

T

TAXIS

Taxis are plentiful at all hotel entrances, but nearly impossible to obtain by the street-side hailing method. You are better off walking up to a hotel, casino or shopper center and hiring one there. Fares are metered and the journey from the Strip to Downtown costs around $15. Calling a cab from a far-flung distance often requires up to an hour-long wait (see also Tipping).

TELEPHONES

The country code for the US is 1; the area code for Clark County (where Las Vegas is located) is 702. While in the Vegas area, calls within the metropolitan vicinity need only the seven-digit number that follows the area code. International calls require 011 + country code + number. Be aware that hotels hike up the price of long distance calls enormously.

TICKETS

Hotels have their own box offices, many of which accept over-the-phone purchases with a credit card. Tickets for some hotel events, as well as most other major events in Las Vegas (concerts, sporting events) can be purchased via **Ticketmaster** at 800-745 3000 or www.ticketmaster.com/lasvegas. Remember, there are surcharges for using ticketing services, so prices will be cheaper if you buy direct from the venue's box office.

TIME DIFFERENCES

The continental US is divided into three time zones; Las Vegas is in the Pacific Time Zone, which is eight hours behind Greenwich Mean Time. Las Vegas operates on Daylight Saving Time; in mid-March, clocks move ahead by one hour, and then fall back by one hour in late October.

TIPPING

Tipping (often called 'tokes' in Las Vegas) is the grease that keeps the machine of Las Vegas operating, far more than in other American cities. Most tourist service employees depend on tips as an important portion of their income. Tipping is simpler and less trouble if you carry a selection of dollars in the $1, $5, and $10 denominations with you for this purpose.

Most tipping is in the $2–5 range, but sometimes a larger tip will help things move along. No table available at a big hotel restaurant for hours? A $10 or $20 bill will usually get you a seat immediately. Valet parking full? Try $5 first, more if it is a holiday or special event, and a space will often magically appear. If at valet pick-up a huge group of people are already waiting for their cars, waits of up to 20 minutes are not uncommon; however, a bill with the right picture on it handed to the ticket taker with a request to speed up the process will almost always have you out pretty quickly. When you tip under these circumstances, do so discreetly.

Restaurant tipping ranges between 15 to 20 percent of the total bill before taxes. A good tipper will go to 25 percent for extraordinary service. Be warned: some restaurants automatically include a 15 percent surcharge for large tables; you may argue the charge if service is poor. If it is included, you may of course add a small percentage for exceptional service. Remember, if service is bad, you are not obligated to tip, but select another server the next time you visit that establishment.

Here are some general suggestions for how much to tip, but when in doubt, always overtip: in Las Vegas, this may improve your vacation immeasurably:

Bartenders: $1–2 per round for two or more

Bellmen: $1–2 per bag

Cocktail Waitresses: $1–2 per round

Concierges: $5 and up, depending on service

Doormen: $1 per bag, $1 for cab call

Limo Drivers: 15 percent of total bill

Maids: $2 per day, left at the end of stay

Pool Attendants: $1

Taxi Drivers: 20 percent

Valet Parking: $2 when car is returned; $5–10 to find a spot on a busy night; $5 to ticket taker for fast return

Wait Staff (Restaurant): 15–20 percent of total before taxes

Wait Staff (Showroom): $5–10

Tipping in Casinos
Change Attendants: 5 percent and up, depending on your luck and their interaction.
Cocktail Waitresses: $1, particularly if the drink is free; tipping with gaming chips is acceptable as well.
Dealers: If you are winning, tip the dealer by placing a bet for him or her, one-half of your bet; when leaving the table in the black, tip according to your conscience.

TOURIST INFORMATION

Contact the **Las Vegas Convention and Visitors Authority** for tourist information at 3150 Paradise Road, Las Vegas, NV 89109, tel: 702-892 7575 or 877-847 4858, www.visitlasvegas.com.

V

VISAS AND ENTRY REQUIREMENTS

All international visitors need passports. Citizens of Canada, Mexico, and most western European nations, as well as Australia, New Zealand, and Japan, can stay for up to 90 days without a visa, as long as they have a valid passport and a return ticket. Others entering the US might need visas.

Adult visitors staying longer than 72 hours may bring along the following items duty free: 1 liter of wine or liquor; 100 cigars (non-Cuban), or 3lbs (1.5kg) of tobacco, or 200 cigarettes; and gifts valued under $100. Absolutely no food (including canned goods) or plants of any type are permissible. Visitors may also arrive and depart with up to $10,000 currency without declaration.

W

WEBSITES AND INTERNET ACCESS

Wireless access is available in most hotels (also in public areas) for free or for an extra daily fee. Some coffee shops and restaurants along the Strip and Downtown also offer free Wi-fi. It is also available in a one-mile radius of the Fremont Street Experience.

Public libraries in Las Vegas offer Internet access at no charge. The Las Vegas Clark County Library is at 833 Las Vegas Boulevard North, tel: 702-734 READ, www.lvccld.org. There are also internet facilities in most hotel business centers, though these can be expensive.

If you want to investigate Las Vegas online before you leave home, the following are some websites to help you do it:

www.visitlasvegas.com The official website of the Las Vegas Visitors and Convention Authority.

www.vegas.com Operated by the parent company of the *Las Vegas Sun*, *Las Vegas Life*, *Las Vegas Weekly*, and countless others, this is perhaps the most comprehensive online source of information about the city.

www.lasvegas.com Another fairly comprehensive site, especially for show tickets and finding out about upcoming events.

www.lasvegasadvisor.com Maintained by one of the city's best resource centers, Las Vegas Advisor is particularly strong on gaming information.

www.lvol.com The Las Vegas Online Entertainment Guide has listings for shows, concerts, and other entertainment.

Y

YOUTH HOSTELS

One of few hostels in town, the **Sin City Hostel** (1208 Las Vegas Boulevard South; tel: 702-868 0222, www.sincityhostel.com) is located between the Strip and Downtown. The neighborhood is not the best, but is safe during the day; be sure to travel in a group – or at least in pairs – at night.

RECOMMENDED HOTELS

There are nearly 150,000 hotel rooms in Las Vegas. This makes selecting accommodations intimidating, but not impossible. Consider the usual factors – cost, location, and budget – as well as how integral you want your hotel to be to your visit. It is possible, though not advisable, to visit Las Vegas and never leave your hotel premises.

The following is a recommended selection of Sin City's best hotels in four price categories. For a comprehensive listing of available hotels and motels, contact the Las Vegas Convention and Visitors Authority (see page 114).

All businesses must comply with the Americans with Disabilities Act, and so are wheelchair accessible. Newer properties are the easiest to navigate, older and Downtown properties can be slightly more difficult.

All hotels accept all major credit cards (including Visa, Mastercard, and American Express), and while room counts include suites, price ranges do not. Expect holiday and weekend rates to be significantly higher, and be sure to ask for specific quotes for your intended stay. Las Vegas hosts a significant number of conventions every year, and when large crowds are in town, hotel prices go up. Always research special packages or deals on offer, as these can cut costs considerably. For more information about most of these hotels, particularly with regard to their casinos and attractions, see page 32.

$$$$	over $200
$$$	$100–$200
$$	$50–$100
$	under $50

STRIP CASINOS AND RESORTS

Aria Resort and Casino $$$$ *3730 Las Vegas Boulevard South, tel: 702-590 7757, toll free: 1-866-359 7757, www.arialasvegas.com.* The theme at this CityCenter hotel is modern. Rooms are sleek and chock-full of technology. Downstairs, the casino has a clean, natural feel. The building has been cited for its environmental sensitivities – definitely not the Vegas of old. 4,004 rooms.

Bally's Las Vegas $$$ *3645 Las Vegas Boulevard South, toll free: 1-877-603 4390,* www.ballyslasvegas.com. Bally's is one of the oldest hotels on the Strip, but also one of the most overlooked. The rooms in its south tower, now named Jubilee Tower, were thoroughly renovated in 2014. The hotel has a beautiful pool area that is perfect for hot days. 2,814 rooms.

Bellagio $$$$ *3600 Las Vegas Boulevard South, tel: 702-693 7111, toll free: 1-888-987 6667,* www.bellagio.com. One of the city's most lavish resorts, Bellagio proves the type of Italian elegance that $1.6 billion can buy. The standard guest rooms are satisfyingly plush, decorated in shades of brown, black, and cream. Be sure to ask for a room overlooking the fountains, as there is in-room music (on the TV) that is choreographed to the water show. 3,933 rooms.

Caesars Palace $$$ *3570 Las Vegas Boulevard South, tel: 702-731 7110, toll free: 1-866-227 5938,* www.caesarspalace.com. A standard-setter since its opening, elegance at Caesars seems within reach of anyone. In excellent accommodations marble and mahogany abound. Baths feature oversize marble tubs and European fixtures, and rooms are tastefully decorated with art and sculpture matching the ancient Roman theme that runs throughout the resort. There is also an expansive pool complex. 3,292 rooms in six towers.

Circus Circus Las Vegas Hotel and Casino $$ *2880 Las Vegas Boulevard South, tel: 702-734 0410, toll free: 1-800-634 3450,* www.circuscircus.com. Circus Circus is Las Vegas's original family-friendly, low-roller hotel-casino. Most rooms have been renovated. Still the name of the game here is budget, although it's done quite playfully, as though you're under the big top. 3,773 rooms.

The Cosmopolitan of Las Vegas $$$ *3708 Las Vegas Boulevard South, tel: 702-698 7000, 702-698 7575,* www.cosmopolitanlasvegas.com. Most casinos spread out; the Cosmopolitan has gone up. This explains the appeal of the open-air balconies that adorn almost every room. Also of note: the Chandelier bar and a host of restaurants. 2,995 rooms

Encore $$$$ *3121 Las Vegas Boulevard South, tel: 702-770 7171, www. encorelasvegas.com.* A sister property to Wynn next door, this hotel features all suites, complete with sitting areas and sumptuous beds. The casino is bright and airy – a rarity in Las Vegas. 2,034 rooms

Excalibur Hotel and Casino $$ *3850 Las Vegas Boulevard South, tel: 702-597 7777, toll free: 1-877-750 5464, www.excalibur.com.* Excalibur offers a Renaissance Faire experience aimed squarely at families and travelers on a budget. Rooms are surprisingly restrained considering the hotel's gaudy castle-like exterior, with wrought-iron accents over dark wood and contemporary touches of red, blue, and green that evokes a medieval fantasy. 3,981 rooms.

Flamingo Las Vegas $$ *3555 Las Vegas Boulevard South, tel: 702-733 3111, www.flamingolasvegas.com.* The Flamingo retains its vintage desert oasis flavor with a large, lush tropical pool and garden area, complete with a wildlife habitat. One of the oldest resorts on the Strip (1946), the Flamingo still manages to hold its own in the middle of all the upstarts. 3,642 rooms.

Four Seasons Hotel Las Vegas $$$$ *3960 Las Vegas Boulevard South, tel: 702-632 5000, toll free: 1-877-632 5000, www.fourseasons.com/las vegas.* The Four Seasons offers quiet, ultra-luxurious accommodations on the upper floors of the Mandalay Bay tower. A large pool set in a lush garden is available only to Four Seasons guests. 424 rooms.

Harrah's Las Vegas $$$ *3475 Las Vegas Boulevard South, tel: toll free: 1-800-214 9110, www.harrahslasvegas.com.* Bright colors, light wood, and brass fixtures lend an upbeat feel to the accommodations in this venerable resort, which has a light, outdoorsy atmosphere reminiscent of Carnivale. Jacuzzi tubs are available. Theme: Carnival. 2,677 rooms.

LINQ Hotel and Casino $$–$$$, *3535 Las Vegas Boulevard South, tel: 702-322 0560, toll free: 800-634 6441, www.caesars.com/linq.* Formerly known as Imperial Palace Las Vegas, it reopened as the LINQ in 2013 after a $223 million renovation. The High Roller, the world's biggest Ferris wheel, draws crowds to the resort. 2,640 rooms.

Luxor Hotel and Casino $$–$$$ *3900 Las Vegas Boulevard South, tel: 702-262 4444, toll free: 1-877-386 4658, www.luxor.com.* The Luxor consists of a 30-story Egyptian pyramid and two towers. The rooms in the pyramid have one sloping glass wall. All rooms feature Art Deco and Egyptian-inspired furnishings with marble bathrooms. Discount rates are often available. 4,407 rooms.

Mandalay Bay Resort and Casino $$$ *3950 Las Vegas Boulevard South, tel: 702-632 7777, toll free: 877-632 7800, www.mandalaybay. com.* Guests at the Mandalay will enjoy an 11-acre (4-hectare) tropical environment, including a wave pool, enormous spa, a shark aquarium, and a number of trendy restaurants, including the House of Blues. Rooms are spacious and designed with a South Pacific motif. 3,309 rooms.

Mandarin Oriental Las Vegas $$$$ *3752 Las Vegas Boulevard South, tel: 702-590 8888, toll free: 1-888-881 9578, www.mandarinoriental. com/lasvegas.* Luxury has a new address in this property, which prides itself on customer service. Rooms are compact but exquisite; the eighth-floor spa is one of the best in the world. 392 rooms

MGM Grand Hotel and Casino $$$ *3799 Las Vegas Boulevard South, tel: 702-891 7777, toll free: 1-877-880 0880, www.mgm grand.com.* A variety of buildings results in a variety of room types, including two-story lofts, mansion-style 'homes' and apartment-style one-bedrooms. All rooms come standard with gilt accents and framed photos of classic film stars, providing the perfect touch for this themed resort. 5,044 rooms.

The Mirage $$$ *3400 Las Vegas Boulevard South, tel: 702-791 7111, toll free: 1-800-374-9000, www.mirage.com.* A lovely Polynesian resort, despite being the oldest of the city's post-1950s additions. The rooms have a distinctive beach resort feel, with subdued neutral colors and gold accents. Most have marbled entries and baths, as well as canopied beds. Though the rooms are somewhat small, they are very pleasant. 3,044 rooms.

Monte Carlo Resort and Casino $$$ *3770 Las Vegas Boulevard South, tel: 702-730 7777, toll free: 1-800-311 8999, www.monte carlo.com.* Striking in its understated European theme, this resort captures an air of popular beauty. The outdoor area is particularly lush. Rooms are classically European in flavor and very comfortable. 2,992 rooms.

New York-New York Las Vegas Hotel and Casino $$$ *3790 Las Vegas Boulevard South, tel: 702-740 6969, toll free: 1-866-815 4365, www.newyorknewyork.com.* Taking theming to its extreme, rooms here are done in styles that relate to the Big Apple. Art Deco is the overall inspiration, with round-top furnishings and inlaid wood galore. On average, the rooms (and their bathrooms) are small, but the overall experience is pleasant. 2,024 rooms.

The Palazzo Resort Hotel Casino $$$ *3325 Las Vegas Boulevard South, tel: 702-607 7777, toll free: 1-866-263 3001, www.palazzo. com.* Much like its sister property, the Venetian, rooms at the Palazzo are suites with sunken living rooms. Great restaurants and a lively casino also are worth visiting. 3,068 rooms.

Paris Las Vegas $$$ *3655 Las Vegas Boulevard South, toll free: 1-877-796 2096, www.parislasvegas.com.* Paris Las Vegas is modeled after the City of Light's Hôtel de Ville, with numerous replicas of Parisian landmarks, including the Eiffel Tower, Rue de la Paix, the Paris Opera House, the Louvre, and the Arc de Triomphe. Rooms are spacious and subtly European. 2,916 rooms.

Planet Hollywood Resort and Casino $$ *3667 Las Vegas Boulevard South, tel: 702-785 5555, toll free: 1-866-919 7472, www. planethollywoodresort.com.* In a former life, this hotel was the Aladdin, but it now has a hip, young ambiance of glass, polished steel, and black tile. Rooms are spacious. 2,659 rooms.

SLS Hotel and Casino Las Vegas $$$ *tel: 702-761-7000, 2535 Las Vegas Boulevard South, http://slslasvegas.com.* Opened in 2014 on the site of legendary Sahara resort, this opulent hotel has rooms designed by famous French designer Philippe Starck and musician Lenny Kravitz. 1,720 rooms.

Stratosphere Casino, Hotel and Tower $$ *2000 Las Vegas Boulevard South, tel: 702-380 7777, www.stratospherehotel.com.* Accommodations are surprisingly comfortable, nicely decorated with Art Deco

DOWNTOWN CASINOS AND RESORTS **137**

touches and black lacquer, and complete with iPod docks. The semi-central location, however – not quite the Strip, not quite Downtown – leaves the Stratosphere out on its own. 2,427 rooms.

TI (Treasure Island) $$–$$$ *3300 Las Vegas Boulevard South, tel: 702-894 7111, toll free: 1-800-944 7444, www.treasureisland.com.* Affordable and comfortable – though not elaborate – rooms are housed in a Y-shaped tower. Rooms face the Strip or look out over the Mirage casino or the mountains. 2,884 rooms.

Tropicana Las Vegas Hotel and Casino $$ *3801 Las Vegas Boulevard South, tel: 702-739 2222, toll free: 1-800-462 8767, www.troplv.com.* Aimed at adult travelers, the hotel is a slice of subtly themed Polynesia – bamboo and wood dominate. Guest rooms are among the largest on the Strip. The tropical pool area (with swim-up blackjack tables) is stark and hip. 1,467 rooms.

The Venetian Resort Hotel Casino $$$ *3355 Las Vegas Boulevard South, tel: 702-414 1000, toll free: 1-866-659 9643, www.venetian.com.* Renaissance Italy is captured in dramatic architecture and land-scaping, including canals with operating gondolas. Rooms are all suites, complete with a sunken living room. 4,027 rooms.

Wynn Las Vegas $$$$ *3131 Las Vegas Boulevard South, tel: 702-770 7000, toll free: 1-877-321 9966, www.wynnlasvegas.com.* Arguably one of the city's most lavish resorts, the Wynn is sultry and sophisticated. From the artificial mountain at its entrance to the lagoons and waterfalls at the back, no expense has been spared to create a luxurious hideaway. Rooms are simple yet decked out with technology. 2,716 rooms.

DOWNTOWN CASINOS AND RESORTS

El Cortez Hotel and Casino $–$$ *600 Fremont Street, tel: 702-385 5200, toll free: 1-800-634 6703, www.elcortezhotelcasino.com.* El Cortez, the city's oldest operating casino (built in 1941), is a centerpiece of the Fremont East Entertainment District. The most pleasant rooms are in the 14-story tower, but the older rooms are still fine. 364rooms.

The D Hotel $$ *301 Fremont Street, tel: 702-388 2400*, www.thed. com. Many rooms in this hotel, formerly known as Fitzgerald's Casino Hotel, offer nice views of the city and mountains within comfortable surroundings. Accommodations are of the standard variety and within a mid-budget price range. Attractive views of the Fremont Street Experience can also be enjoyed in this (mostly) low-roller haven. 638 rooms.

Four Queens Hotel and Casino $$ *202 Fremont Street, tel: 702-385 4011, toll free: 1-800-634 6045*, www.fourqueens.com. A neon landmark since 1966, the Four Queens today entices mainly older guests. Rooms are of Southwestern or earth-tone decor and are pleasant and affordable. On-site restaurants include Hugo's Cellar, an always-busy classic with an award-winning wine list. 690 rooms.

Fremont Hotel and Casino $$ *200 East Fremont Street, tel: 702-385 3232, toll free: 1-800-634 6182*, www.fremontcasino.com. Constructed in 1956 as Las Vegas's first high-rise building, the Fremont's guest rooms are comfortable, modern, and decorated in a tropical-floral style. The hotel hosts many Hawaiian travelers and the Second Street Grill features Pacific Rim specialties. 447 rooms.

Golden Gate Hotel and Casino $ *1 Fremont Street, tel: 702-385 1906, toll free: 1-800-426 1906*, www.goldengatecasino.com. This charmingly old-fashioned operation is the city's oldest hotel. Its small (120 sq ft/12 sq m) rooms, with plaster walls and mahogany doors, were renovated at the end of last decade but still hark back to another era. Rates are low and the location at the west end of the Fremont Street Experience couldn't be better. 106 rooms.

Golden Nugget Hotel $$$ *129 East Fremont Street, tel: 702-385 7111, toll free: 1-800-634 3454*, www.goldennugget.com. The 1946 Golden Nugget is the jewel of Downtown; metropolitan elegance supersedes the surrounding glitz. Accommodations – including the Rush Tower – are luxurious. The pool area, dubbed the Tank, is exceptional; a water slide shoots swimmers through a shark tank. 2,419rooms.

Main Street Station Casino, Brewery and Hotel $$ *200 North Main Street, tel: 702-387 1896, toll free: 1-800-465 0711,* www.mainstreet casino.com. Main Street Station is Las Vegas's best-kept secret, as the Victorian-styled casino is filled with expensive antiques. Rooms are spacious, quiet, and simply decorated, with shutters instead of drapes. Dining options include several very good restaurants. 406 rooms.

Plaza Hotel and Casino $ *1 Main Street, tel: 702-386 2110, toll free: 1-800-634 6575,* www.plazahotelcasino.com. A few steps from the Greyhound bus station, this high-rise hotel has its own wedding chapel as well as exercise facilities, a swimming pool, several restaurants, a concierge desk, cable TV, and even its own shuttle to the airport. Rooms are a great value for the price. 1,003 rooms.

OFF-STRIP CASINOS AND RESORTS

Aliante Casino and Hotel $$ *Aliante Parkway, tel: 702-692 7777, toll free: 1-877-477 7627,* www.aliantecasinohotel.com. This hotel sits inside the Aliante master-planned community, far from the Strip but close to the mountains and the Las Vegas Motor Speedway. Rooms are spacious and modern with floor-to-ceiling windows (some of which gaze upon the Strip). On-site restaurants are well-regarded. 211 rooms.

Boulder Station Hotel and Casino $$ *4111 Boulder Highway, tel: 702-432 7777, toll free: 1-800-638 2846,* www.boulderstation.com. Located on the Boulder Strip going out of town, the Boulder Station Hotel offers a small-scale version of the inclusive upscale resort. Rooms are comfortable and attractive, but a bit higher-priced than you might expect this far off the Strip. 300 rooms.

Gold Coast Hotel and Casino $ *4000 West Flamingo Road, tel: 702-367-7111, toll free: 1-888-402 6278,* www.goldcoastcasino.com. The Gold Coast Hotel, located one mile (1.5km) west of the Strip, offers a combination of entertainment and gaming, as well as a bowling center, three lounges, a dance hall, and a theater. Guest rooms are both comfortable and affordable. 711 rooms.

Hard Rock Hotel and Casino $$$ *4455 Paradise Road, tel: 702-693 5000, toll free: 1-473 7625,* www.hardrockhotel.com. A surprising exercise in casual elegance, the Hard Rock's rooms are spacious and pleasing, decorated in a classic Modernist style. Light fixtures made of cymbals adorn the ceilings. The tower is all suites. 1,505 rooms.

Orleans Hotel and Casino $ *4500 West Tropicana Avenue, tel: 702-365 7111, toll free: 1-800-675 3267,* www.orleanscasino.com. The guest rooms here come standard with separate sitting areas, and are often an excellent bargain. They are lavishly appointed, with decor in brass, antiques, and lace, evoking the Big Easy's classic ambiance. 1,886 rooms.

Palace Station Hotel and Casino $$ *2411 West Sahara Avenue, tel: 702-367 2411, toll free: 1-800-634 3101,* www.palacestation.com. Located just off the Strip near Interstate 15, the Palace Station's best rooms are within the tower, built in 1991, while original rooms are in a two-story building surrounding the pool. If possible, request one of the corner rooms, which have larger bathrooms. 1,030 rooms.

Palms Casino Resort $$$ *4321 West Flamingo Road, tel: 702-942 7777, toll free: 1-866-942 7770,* www.palms.com. A favorite haunt of locals and celebrities alike, the Palms offers two towers of luxury rooms and suites, as well as a recording studio and one of Las Vegas's top concert venues. Nightclubs on-site include Ghostbar and the Rojo Lounge. 702 rooms.

Red Rock Casino Resort and Spa $$ *11011 West Charleston, tel: 702-797 7777, toll free: 1-866-767 7773,* www.redrocklasvegas.com. Far from the Strip but convenient for Red Rock Canyon and Mount Charleston, this ultra-elegant spa resort features attractive packages, as well as a host of great restaurants. 818 rooms.

Rio All-Suite Hotel and Casino $$ *3700 West Flamingo Road, tel: 702-252 7777, toll free: 1-866-746 7671,* www.riolasvegas.com. The Rio is a long walk (or a short cab ride) to the Strip, but has received international acclaim as one of the city's best values. Every room here is a suite, and they rank as some of the largest in town. Decor is a blend of bold colors and wood. 2,522 rooms.

Sam's Town Hotel and Gambling Hall $$ *5111 Boulder Highway, tel: 702-456 7777, toll free: 1-800-634 6371,* www.samstownlv.com. The rustic Wild West and Native American decor may sound kitschy, but rooms here are actually quiet, comfortable, and attractive. The real treat is the nine-story atrium over Mystic Falls Indoor Park, complete with live trees, running water, and footpaths, which also features free daily laser-light and water shows. Some in-facing rooms below the ninth floor are within this atrium. 646 rooms.

Sunset Station Hotel and Casino $$ *1301 West Sunset Road, tel: 702-547 7777, toll free: 1-888-786 7389*, www.sunsetstation.com. The Mediterranean interior of Sunset Station is stunning. Amenities include a 13-screen movie theatre, bowling alley and KidsQuest indoor play area, making this a sure-fire family winner. Sunset Station is located in Green Valley, across from a major shopping area. 457 rooms.

MOTELS

Howard Johnson $–$$ *165 East Tropicana Avenue, tel: 702-476 6500, toll free: 1-800-221 5801*, www.hojo.com. Within walking distance to the Strip, this pet-friendly motel has a pool and free Wi-fi.

Motel 6 $ *195 East Tropicana Avenue, tel: 702-798 0728*, www.motel 6.com. Three blocks from the Strip and not far from the airport, this motel has a swimming pool, a food store, and plenty of parking.

INDEX

Berlitz POCKET GUIDE

LAS VEGAS

Fourteenth edition 2016

Editor: Rachel Lawrence
Authors: James P. Reza and Matthew R. Poole
Head of Production: Rebeka Davies
Picture Editor: Tom Smyth
Cartography Update: Carte
Update Production: AM Services
Photography Credits: Abraham Nowitz/Apa Publications 13, 30, 52, 53, 54/55, 77, 80, 81, 93, 100, 106; Al Argueta/Apa Publications 34/35, 37, 43, 69, 81, 89, 99; ARIA 105, 107; Getty Images 14, 16, 19, 21, 22, 25, 28, 33, 49, 58, 60, 61, 78, 83, 85, 86, 90, 91, 94, 97; iStock 4TC, 4MC, 4ML, 4TL, 5T, 5TC, 5M, 5MC, 5M, 6MC, 6ML, 6ML, 6TL, 7M, 7T, 7M, 7TC, 8L, 8R, 9, 9R, 11, 23, 26, 47, 56, 63, 64, 68, 70, 74, 79, 82, 84 ; Richard Nowitz/Apa Publications 40, 51, 59, 66, 102; Shutterstock 5MC, 6TL, 38, 39, 44/45, 46, 50, 72
Cover Picture: Robert Harding

Distribution

UK: Dorling Kindersley Ltd,
A Penguin Group company, 80 Strand, London, WC2R 0RL; sales@uk.dk.com
United States: Ingram Publisher Services, 1 Ingram Boulevard, PO Box 3006, La Vergne, TN 37086-1986; ips@ingramcontent.com
Australia and New Zealand: Woodslane, 10 Apollo St, Warriewood, NSW 2102, Australia; info@woodslane.com.au
Worldwide: Apa Publications (Singapore) Pte, 7030 Ang Mo Kio Avenue 5, 08-65 Northstar @ AMK, Singapore 569880 apasin@singnet.com.sg

All Rights Reserved
© 2016 Apa Digital (CH) AG and
Apa Publications (UK) Ltd

Printed in China by CTPS

Berlitz®

speaking your language

phrase book & dictionary
phrase book & CD

Available in: Arabic, Brazilian Chinese, Croatian, Czech*, Danish German, Greek, Hebrew*, Hindi* Korean, Latin American Spanish, Norwegian, Polish, Portuguese, Turkish, Vietnamese
*Book only

... Burmese*, Cantonese*
..., English Filipino, Finnish*...
..., Indonesian, Italian, Japanese
... Mandarin Chinese, Mexican...
... Russian, Spanish, Swedish...